PROPHECY
2022
and Beyond

The Butterfly in the Hurricane

Book Titles by Betsey Lewis

Stargates
Extraterrestrial Encounters of The Extraordinary Kind
2021 Looking into the Future
2020 Prophecies and Predictions
Star Beings
Déjà vu
Ancient Serpent Gods
Mystic Revelations of Seven
Mystic Revelations of Thirteen
Baffled by Their Brilliance
Prophecy 2016 and Beyond: The Prophets Speak
Earth Energy: Return to Ancient Wisdom
Communicating with the Other Side
Angels, Aliens and Prophecy II

Spiritual Books for Children
Alexander Phoenix
The Story of Rainbow Eyes
A Worm Named Sherm

PROPHECY
2022
and Beyond

The Butterfly in the Hurricane

Betsey Lewis

Prophecy 2022 and Beyond: The Butterfly in the Hurricane

(3-27)

Copyright © 2022 Betsey Lewis

ISBN: 979-8528405582

Cover design by Betsey Lewis

There are those who are skeptics. There are those who are doubters. And there are those who prefer to don rose-colored glasses. To these ones, I have no words; for they have made their choice, though the signs have been many.

There are those who have gentle stirrings. And there are those who have stepped upon the beautiful threshold of awareness—all on the verge of perceiving that which is there to see. To these ones, I say, open your exquisite senses. Look with fine clarity into that which is beyond and beneath, within and without. In these coming critical times, listen to and heed the directive of your spirits that retain the high wisdom you are now perceiving.

Lastly, there are those who know. There are those who, within their tender hearts, have seen, felt, and recognized that which is there to see. To these ones, I have no words, for they already know the Words—ancient wisdom words that have stood eternal and pure since they were first given, ever triumphantly surviving the vulgar ravages of time.

—Mary Summer Rain, Phoenix Rising—No-Eyes' Vision of the Changes to Come

Prophecy 2022

Prophecy 2022

CONTENTS

	Acknowledgements	i
Chapter 1	The Agenda	3
Chapter 2	Atlantis Returned	17
Chapter 3	Covid–Mass Psychosis	21
Chapter 4	The New Religion	31
Chapter 5	Satanism	37
Chapter 6	The Moon and Mars	55
Chapter 7	Planet X	63
Chapter 8	Wisdom of the Indigenous	75
Chapter 9	All Lives Matter	83
Chapter 10	Presidential Race 2024	89
Chapter 11	The War on Ascension	105
Chapter 12	Earth Changes	111
Chapter 13	Nesara and Med Beds	117
Chapter 14	Prophets and Psychics	121
Chapter 15	The Matrix	125
Chapter 16	The Power of Aum or Om	133
Chapter 17	Chemtrails	147
Chapter 18	More Predictions	155
Chapter 19	Extraterrestrials Among Us	167
Chapter 20	Honoring Earth & All Life	179
Chapter 21	Afterword	211
	Dear Future Generations	215
	Bibliography	219
	About the Author	221

Prophecy 2022

ACKNOWLEDGMENTS

To the Seers, the Teachers, the Healers, and the Wisdom Keepers of the ages who come and go like blazing comets across the starlit skies—thank you for giving humanity valuable wisdom and glimpses into an ever-changing future.

Prophecy 2022

"It is hard for me to understand a culture that not only hates and fights his brothers but even attacks Nature and abuses her. Man must love all creation, or he will love none of it. Love is something you and I must have. We must have it because our spirit feeds upon it. Without it, our courage fails. Without love, we can no longer look out confidently at the world. Instead, we turn inwardly and begin to feed upon our own personalities and little by little we destroy ourselves." —Chief Dan George

CHAPTER ONE

THE AGENDA

The Year 2022 or Year Zero has arrived. Number 22 is a master number. It is the Master Builder. It holds great power and can be used for good or evil. Twenty-two brings together the spiritual and the material. 2022 is also the Chinese Year of the Tiger which means it will be a year of sudden major changes. 2022 will be a year of risk-taking and the beginning of revolutionary changes. Will the Family of Light win or will the Family of Dark succeed in their evil plan to control the world? It's going to be a fight—like the one fought thousands of years ago in Atlantis by the two opposing groups, but I sense the worm beginning to turn against the dark forces. There are currently millions of the Family of Light members on Earth, and light is returning to this planet where those of the Dark have fed off our emotions of fear, negativity, war, and greed; because this is a free-will universe, and all has been allowed. It's time for all of us to stand against tyranny taking over our world and our nation and reject those who would destroy it in order to usher in their cultural Marxist tyranny.

Our planet is at the end of a 75,000-year cycle and we are in the midst of a dimensional shift. Events will happen during this period that has never occurred in the recorded history of humankind. Weather changes and increased natural disasters are part of this shift. Because the earth is graduating, if we don't upgrade during this lifetime, we may have to repeat hundreds or thousands of additional lifetimes. It may take souls on Earth now thousands of years to return to Earth.

Before writing this book, I went through an extreme amount of soul-searching, research, and meditation to view the future. I know that we have a choice of two paths to take. One road leads to our extinction and the other leads to a glorious future.

It was December 2019, I experienced a vision of flu hitting America, and I heard the words Spanish Flu. I sensed it would take hold in 2021, but at the time, I didn't realize the enormity of my premonition that a flu virus would become a pandemic known as COVID-19 that would rage around the world. Already COVID-19 has taken 5 million lives, young and old, worldwide, and there is no end in sight as variants take hold. The Delta variant began in India in 2020 but took hold in America in 2021 and by late November 2021, WHO (World Health Organization) warned of a new COVID-19 variant detected in South Africa. The new variant contains more mutations to the spike protein, the component of the virus that binds to cells, than the highly contagious delta variant. The new variant has been deemed by WHO as Omicron. Omicron is a Greek word meaning small.

Pandora's Box was opened in 2019 and all the evil came pouring out upon the Earth. The virus wasn't an accident.

There are many agendas afoot, but the 2022 agenda for humanity has been in the works for a long time. A spiritual war is taking place on Earth between the Family of Light and the Family of Dark, warring extraterrestrials—and others who want to dominate the world at any cost even if that includes the deaths of millions of souls to achieve their evil plan. This is a time when the United States and throughout the world countries fall to demonic influences in 2022 if we don't awaken now.

A spiritual and religious war has begun as more as our democracy and freedoms are taken away from us in the United States and throughout the world. It's all by design. In one year, the United States of America is no longer a free democratic country—there are current mask and vaccines mandates signed into law by President Biden, and those who don't follow the Marxist rules will pay dearly by the Left as we witnessed with people imprisoned without a trial, adult and children's books banned, people ostracized for not getting the mandated COVID-19 vaccines, the cost of living has doubled, gasoline, and just about everything under the sun has gone up. Inflation is now over 7%. Since 2021 over million illegal immigrants from Haiti, Afghanistan, Mexico, Central America, and the Mideast have flooded our U.S. borders. Thousands of illegal migrant children have been secretly flown to major U.S. cities in the middle of the night and loaded on buses to other destinations. Are their children going to be used in sex trafficking? Thousands of people are walking off their jobs, protesting against Biden's vaccine mandates being pushed on everyone, including small children and pregnant women.

The unvaccinated have become "white supremacists" or the lepers of society if they don't take Kool-Aid COVID vaccines known to have horrible side effects. Oddly, it's the vaccinated that are having COVID-19 breakthroughs, even with the new variant Omicron, which has spread rapidly around the world. If you don't get vaccinated you can't attend concerts, eat at restaurants, get a job or keep your job, and eventually, you won't be able to fly. You are an outcast.

In my book, *2021 Looking into the Future prophecy,* I wrote how deeply troubled I was knowing that those who speak out against tyranny will be silenced. I knew that after Biden was elected, perhaps illegally in a voter election fraud, we would witness something very dark spreading across America and throughout the world. The Family of Dark knows the gullibility of humanity and planned the takeover a long ago while we were comatose to their spreading agenda. Some sensed what was beginning to rear its ugly head years ago, but others were too involved in bashing Trump on major news networks, social media, and newspapers.

We heard from Biden, Pelosi, Democrats, and the media mob how Donald Trump caused the January 6, 2021 riots now called an "Insurrection." Trump never told the crowd on January 6 to riot—ever! But he could have told them to stop, but who would have stopped. Stranger still are the people who appeared in

MAGA clothes, encouraging the Trump crowd to riot. Another man, Ray Epps, also believed to be a Federal Agent, was encouraging people to riot, and those Trump supporters realized what Epps was doing and yelled out "Fed!! Fed!" Another man, perhaps a Fed, was handing out weapons to MAGA supporters. Capitol police told people to go beyond the barriers and into the Capitol building. These people have never been arrested like so many Trump supporters and that's because they were hired to create the riot that happened. Yes, it was planned by the LEFT!!! It was an afront against over 80 million people who either voted for Trump or supported him.

The Democratic Left and biased news like CNN drummed into the easily controlled minds of the public that what happened on that day was an Insurrection compared to Pearl Harbor or the Civil War as if most Americans were that stupid and uneducated that they didn't know that 2,403 military and civilians died on December 7, 1941, in Honolulu, Hawaii when the Japanese bombed Pearl Harbor, or that over 750,000 Confederate and Federal Union (the North) soldiers fought against each other in one of the bloodiest battles in the United States from April 12, 1861, to May 9, 1865. The Federal Union fought to stop black slavery in this country and won.

What an insult to the United States servicemen and women who lost their lives at Pearl Harbor during World War II and in the Civil War. How dare Democratic Senate Majority Leader Chuck Schumer and other politicians compare January 6, 2021, to Pearl Harbor during World War II?

The definition of an Insurrection is the violent attempt to take control of a government. But if January 6 was Insurrection, it was a poorly planned one. Thousands attended the rally for Trump, ordinary people who felt that the 2020 election was dishonest, and Trump should have won. They were not there to take over the government but to support Trump and protest the election.

According to the D.C. Medical Examiner's Office, two civilians died of natural causes, a third died from amphetamine intoxications, and a fourth person was 35-year-old Ashli Babbitt, who was unarmed and shot in the back as she climbed into a broken window leading to the Capital Chamber by a black Capitol Police Officer named Michael Byrd, who became a hero to the Left. How sick is that? In an interview, Byrd said he could not see Babbitt hands and didn't know if she was armed or not, but he shot and killed her anyway.

Did you know that Ashli Babbitt tried to stop the attack on the Capitol Speaker's Lobby, according to video footage of January 6, 2021? Frame-by-frame video evidence analyzed paints a vastly different picture of Babbitt's actions than that portrayed by the media accounts over the past year. They claimed she was "violent," a "rioter," or an "insurrectionist" who was angrily trying to breach the Speaker's Lobby when she was shot. Another footage shot by John Sullivan, also known as Jayden X, shows that Babbitt tried to stop the violence against the Speaker's Lobby at least four times before climbing into a broken window where she was fatally shot.

The media demonized her for their own gain, and that was evil. Ashli served 14 years in the military.

Will the Family of Light win or will the Family of Dark succeed in their evil plan to control the world? It's going to be a fight—like the one fought thousands of years ago in Atlantis by the two opposing groups, but I sense the worm beginning to turn against the dark forces. There are currently millions of Family of Light members on Earth, causing light to return to this planet where those of the Dark have fed off our emotions of fear, negativity, war, and greed. It's because this is a free-will universe, and all has been allowed. It's time for all of us to stand against tyranny taking over our world and our nation and reject those who would destroy it to usher in their cultural Marxist tyranny.

Roger Stone, a conservative consultant, a friend of Donald Trump, and lobbyist for the Republican party said this about CNN and how they once aired part of his prior speech before the events of January 6 at the Capitol about his "apocalyptic views" of politics today.

Stone replied, "Yes, I think it's a struggle between dark and light, between good and evil, between the godly and the godless. And they said, well, that was the inciting of violence. No. That's a statement of my beliefs." He added that other media outlets showed photographs of him with the Proud Boys members with CNN claiming that he was to blame via "guilt-by-association." The major media lied about Stone and what he said the day before on January 5, and they lied about Stone's association with the Proud Boys.

Events are moving very fast, but we still have a choice. We will have to push back hard for our freedom and speak up for our rights. I don't mean a physical fight; I mean a spiritual fight. Stand up for your belief in democracy and freedom of speech and don't let the ignorant and bullies intimidate you.

For a long time, our reality has been engineered into a frequency and pattern of a downward spiral into the darker and heavier energies that are at the lower end of the scale in which the human body can exist. This was not a plan conceived on a moment's notice. It has been put together over eons of time. However, because their plans are counter to creation and God's plan for the Universe, we can upend their final plans for control.

You are probably wondering how this rebellion was allowed to continue to this point? As I mentioned earlier, the freewill aspect is what has been exploited as the basis for their ability to manipulate humanity to be the vehicle of their power. They know that humanity is malleable enough to be influenced and controlled. Mass mind-control has been used through television, cell phones, advertising, and corrupt social media. Young minds have been inundated with false stories and lies. It's a game of bait and switch to keep you in constant confusion.

Biden said he wanted to unite the country before he was elected, but all he has done has caused anger, hatred, violent protests, and a great division. President Biden told us no mask mandates or vaccine mandates in the beginning and now mandates exist for nearly everyone in the United State, whether you want it or not.

Deception is an ancient tool that is only effective because we choose denial rather than facing the implications of what is obvious. We must learn to trust our feeling, our intuition, and then we will be able to disguise the truth from false information when presented to us. How far must the lies and deceit continue until humanity gets what is being perpetrated on them?

The method of producing mass trauma to control humans has been used time and time again throughout history by great leaders but still, we don't learn from the past. There's always an enemy to hate and in 2020 and 2021—COVID-19, the unvaccinated, white supremacists (whoever they are) and former President Trump. It's the old ploy used to foster fear and intentionally to create anger, hate, and chaos to divide us and conquer the innate power within each of us.

Never underestimate your own personal power to transform the world. As you emerge from your cocoons into beautiful butterflies taking to the sky with your newfound freedom, your probable choices with increase. The best way to operate at this time is to be keepers of your own frequency and not go around converting or saving others. Keep yourself open to other views and don't remain rigid in your thoughts. If you don't bend in the wind, you will break.

The Family of Dark has long known that the human spirit is powerful and complex, but also creative and peace-loving. Wars and violence must therefore be created, as we are suddenly seeing with Biden talking about sending U.S. troops to the Ukraine borders to protect Ukraine against Russia.

The frequency of fear must change, and we can do that by changing our thoughts of fear and disaster to positive intent and visualization to change the vibratory pattern. It won't be easy, but it can be done if we mass together and stop hating each other for our differences. If we also stop listening to the propaganda on television, radio, and social media. The Family of Dark has worked out ways to create this downward vibration into heavier energy rather than lifting of vibration as was intended. When extreme fear is created *en masse*, the vibration is like a multitude of nuclear weapons traveling into the ethers and dimensional planes of reality. They seek the darker entities that surround our world and delve into satanic rituals they have used for centuries. This control happens when the mass consciousness of that vibratory level of planetary experience has its focus on experiences at the lowest level of our reality.

We are in a critical test to learn how to control our energy. Will you believe what you are told and not question the motives behind words from our leaders? It's about learning from all energies and choosing this era to live and create a cosmic vibration throughout the universe of LIGHT.

If you listen carefully to all the news media (there are a few exceptional news channels) they repeat the same words over and over to convince you of their lies, and it works. Project MKUltra was the illegal human experimentation program designed and undertaken by the U.S. Central Intelligence Agency that began in 1953 and continued for several decades. Those who want to destroy us, use mind control against us without us even suspecting. It is shown in television ads, the television news, on social media, in video games, on cell phones and it's aimed at the youngest of minds—innocent children.

The World programmers know that creating a prime event such as President John Kennedy's assassination and September 11, 2001, would create a ripple in the time continuum and alter the future. Prime Events don't need to be horrible or evil events, they can be positive and a huge world-altering event.

What would a positive Prime Event be? Remember in the 1977 Spielberg's movie, *Close Encounters of the Third Kind,* where researchers arrive in India to hear thousands of holy people chanting the sound that they heard from the ETs and pointing up to the sky? They were creating a massive positive uplifting vibration like it was done in the Bible when Joshua brought down the walls of Jericho by instructing the Israelites to march once each day for six days and seven times on the seventh day blowing their trumpets.

What if millions of people, on a designated day and time, began chanting Om or Aum? Om is a sacred sound considered by many ancient philosophical texts to be the sound of the universe, encompassing all other sounds within it. If it is the sound of the universe, it is the sound of God. I write more about OM or Aum in another chapter.

Here's the good news. There is a point at which their restrictive pressure of controlling the thought processes of the mass consciousness of the planet can backfire and cause exactly the opposite of what they have planned. This will cause them to panic, and that seems to be what is taking place. They are going to bear down on us in 2022 because they know that we've had it with their dark agenda.

They are so confident that their dark agenda will succeed, but they have forgotten about the *Butterfly in the Hurricane,* where mass consciousness of higher evolved beings come together in thought and prayer and change the intended outcome which would be the culling of the herd and control of those who survive.

While we sit by and watch the Constitution being torn away from us, things will continue to escalate until there is an awakening to the real story. The Truth is that there are multiple levels of activity behind what appears to be a play of incredible magnitude. What the Family of Dark has decided is to put forth is not in harmony with the Creator.

What is your responsibility? It is time you awaken to change the destination of the path that you have taken in the past one hundred years. We must now move into a creative stance, not a resistive posture. Humanities history has been analyzed and studied by minds and computer models to the point that we are known. Every reaction has been studied to the cellular level. We are now faced with our extermination unless we can make a cosmic leap to a level of creative imagination that will nullify their evil plan.

Crying to Jesus, Buddha, Mohammed or God will not help. We have allowed this evil to take place and so each of you collectively must take it upon yourselves to find a solution to their horrible plan. A new consciousness must take place. Of course, not everyone will want to get on board for the change. Many will stick their ostrich heads in the sand and say it's conspiracy theories or plain nonsense. They will grovel in their victimhood, and so be it—let them! But there will come a day when those who have scoffed at what is happening will have an epiphany of the truth. Truth is lighter than darkness, and it will rise to the top.

You are collectively writing the lines to history and the outcome. There is not a moment to waste. If we accomplish this goal and end this chapter of planetary experience, those who have chosen to mock the Creator's plan must be stopped. We cannot leave this change in the hands of others. It's too great a responsibility to be left to a few. Those of you reading this must add your contribution to creating a new matrix, a new paradigm in the timeline.

You and I are faced with the possibility of extinction unless we can make a cosmic leap to a level of creative imagination that will nullify their evil plans. Can we not come together into creative discussion groups and asked for entry into Prime Creator's mind, the one who created us? As the Bible says, "Where two or more of you are gathered together in my Name, there I am also."

Open your eyes and see what is happening all around you. Then you must come to the unpleasant understanding that you have allowed this travesty to occur because systematic deception influenced you. In the worst-case scenario, things might need to get really tough, before the tough get going and you are finally awakened from your deep slumber of deception.

Why do you think the Family of Dark uses words over and over about world situations? It's not to enlighten you, but to control you through words. Here is wisdom—look at the ones who constantly blame others but are more guilty than the ones they condone! It's called smoke and mirrors or hoodwinking, and it means believing in the illusion before you.

How do you change what is destined to be oblivion? Mass consciousness and mass awakening are the keys here. Using physical force will only make matters worse as indicated by the events of January 6, 2021, where people were incarcerated for attending the Trump rally and not even protesting. Some of the participants are still in solitary confinement in filthy jails and other deplorable conditions. Some have been beaten, and still, they have not had their day in court. Aren't we innocent until proven guilty according to the law of the land? Obviously, not in our current world. As it stands now, we are automatically proven guilty without a judge and jury. Is that the new American way! This is Marxism and what a totalitarian government looks like.

I have often referred to time traveler John Titor in my books. John claimed to be an internet blogger in the year 2000 from the future year 2036. He discussed how time travel was invented in his reality of time and how to build a time machine invented in his timeline. He discussed what the world looked like after the second Civil War in America and World War III which involved a nuclear exchange.

John claimed that timelines can change and change every time he jumped into his past. What if there are large number of time travelers, often mistaken for aliens, which visit our timeline to change it. John was asked if some sort of new world government was in place by 2011. And John's response was, "On my worldline, in 2011, the United States is in the middle of a civil war that has dramatic effects on most of the Western governments."

He said the civil war was started by politicians, but he should have included the major news media. John referred to our current society and seemed to see our world as beyond help when he stated, "Have you considered that your society might be better off if half of you were dead? While you sit by and watch your Constitution being torn away from you, you willfully eat poisoned food, buy manufactured products no one needs, and turn an uncaring eye away from millions of people suffering and dying all around you. Is this the 'Universal Law' you subscribe to? Perhaps I should let you all in on a little secret. No one likes you in the future. This time is looked at as being full of lazy, self-centered, civically ignorant sheep. Perhaps you should be less concerned about me and more concerned about that."

Humans have become lazy and obese. No one wants to return to work as witnessed by all the Help Wanted signs across the United States. People are causing mayhem on airline flights with their anger, frustration, and drinking on flights. Drugs have inundated our country and that was done ages ago with our government's knowledge. Some of the people you have voted for have backed cartels. Heroin, Fentanyl, Meth, and prescribed opioids are killing thousands and the homeless. Nearly 841,000 died from 1999 through 2019. Twenty-two people out of every 100,000 died from drug overdoses in 2019 in the US. Opioids were involved in 70.6% (nearly 50,000) of the nearly 71,000 deaths in 2019.

Even if John wasn't a time traveler, he had the foresight to see what humanity was becoming. Whoever John Titor was, he was right about humans and what we have become in the twenty-first century. The world I grew up in was different. People were kinder and more caring; life was a little slower and everything seemed brighter. Food tasted better, the air smelled cleaner, and we were better off without cell phones or the internet. No chemtrails were covering our skies from unmarked jets dropping God knows what on us. Of course, bullies existed, but not like the ones today who seem to have no conscience and wish people dead. The internet has given bullies a mouthpiece to be cruel and hateful.

Numbers of teens are committing suicide because of lockdowns and because of someone's cruel, thoughtless, hurtful words that appear on social media about them. In some instances, a bully encourages a young teen to commit suicide because they didn't deserve to live. Those bullies who harm others will pay in a big way, if not in this life, they will in their next incarnation. Karma is a cosmic boomerang!

People have written to me and asked how can I change the world. As the Dalai Lama said, "If you think you are too small to make a difference, try sleeping with a mosquito."

This is not a time to hide and use the usual excuse of "What can one person do." A large number of "one persons" can accomplish a great deal. Using violence and guns is not the way to do it. Subtle energy and words are powerful like a small wave that builds to become a tsunami upon the ocean.

Humans are addicted to TV, cell phones, movies, and soul-jarring music, all lower vibrations. Anything that is said on major news stations is believed, and large numbers of Americans believe that what politicians and major news tell them as if they could never lie to us, but they do all the time.

Do not dwell on the negative events planned for humanity but turn your thoughts to what it is that you would like to experience on this planet at this time and become the power of the Butterfly in the Hurricane. Certain Indigenous shamans have been known to create rain merging with everything in nature and becoming rain. The ego is gone. This is about the sacred connection between humans and the land. Instead of fighting the elements, they become the elements!

Here's a reminder of what human thought can do with our planet's electrical grid. On September 11, 2001, two National Oceanic and Atmospheric Administrations (NOAA) space weather satellites known as GOES-8, and GOES 10 that monitor the Earth's magnetic field picked up a huge spike during the attack on the World Trade buildings. Here's the remarkable part of this event—GOES-8 was orbiting 22,300 miles above the Earth, traveling around the equator on that day. The satellite detected the first surge that topped out at nearly 50 united (nano testlas) higher than any reading previously recorded. The time was 9 a.m. eastern standard time, 15 minutes after the first plane hit the World Trade Center and about 15 minutes before the second impact.

Every living being on Earth has consciousness and that consciousness is connected to all of life. When you are disconnected from your conscious thinking, you become an unwitting participant in mind control manipulations. This purposefully designed reality of fear and chaos distracts your attention away from the massive spiritual awakening that defines these times.

When we ignore the past, history repeats itself, playing out age-old dramas in different eras of time. Some will close their eyes to reality and says it's all conspiracy theories, but there will come a time when they awaken from their slumber, realize the horrible things being perpetrated on humanity.

The Butterfly Effect is the theory that a butterfly's wings can set off a string of escalating events that can lead to the formation of a hurricane. Until humans realize how powerful we can be united, we will be tossed around in the violent wind without direction, or we will create the hurricane and control the outcome. It's our choice!

Betsey Lewis

CHAPTER TWO

ATLANTIS RETURNED

They say that there is nothing new under the sun and that history repeats itself. It appears that is a fact that we are reliving Atlantis in its last days here in the United States and throughout the world. We are the Atlanteans who returned to stop tyranny and slavery.

At least 10,000 years ago, the great continent of Atlantis existed and began to break up according to the great sleeping seer Edgar Cayce. Legends were written. The Athenian philosopher Plato, who lived during the classic period in ancient Greece, introduced Atlantis in 360 BC in Timaeus. Plato wrote that there were beings half God and half-human. They created a Utopian Civilization and became a great naval power.

According to Cayce's readings, the size of Atlantis was about the size of Europe. The continent had gone through three major periods of division—the first two took place around 15,600 B.C.E. when the mainland was divided into islands. The three main islands were named Poseida, Og, and Aryan.

Like our world today, Atlantis had reached the pinnacle of power and technology. Edgar Cayce (March 18, 1877 – Jan. 3, 1945) gave thousands of readings in a trance-like state to individual souls who had one or more incarnations in Atlantis and reincarnated in America in the present time. Along with the advanced technological abilities, Atlanteans were extremists. Sound familiar? Cayce said that they exhibited individual and group karma associated with selfishness and exploitation where others were concerned.

Many of the souls he read for lived during one of the periods of destruction or geological changes in Atlantean history. If Cayce's prophecies are correct, a similar period of Earth changes is upon us.

Atlantis didn't disappear into the ocean in a single day but over years. There was enough warning for the Atlantean people to escape to Europe, Africa, Egypt, and the Americas. Their pyramidal structures were built in honor of Atlantis and still stand today as a reminder of the past.

Why did Cayce say that Atlantean incarnations have exerted so much influence on individuals, especially in our time? He said this during one of his trance readings No. 364-1:

"Be it true that there is the fact of reincarnation, and that souls that once occupied such an environment (Atlantis) are entering the Earth's sphere and inhabiting individuals in the present (and in our time). Is it any wonder that if they made such alterations in the affairs of Earth in their day, as to bring destruction upon themselves—if they are entering now, they might make many changes in the affairs of peoples and individuals in the present?"

Faults and mistakes once recognized can be corrected, and America may yet be spared the fate that overtook Atlantis from their greed and corruption.

In Atlantis, scientists were experimenting with genes and DNA and created half-animal and half-human beings that we believe were only myths. Where do you think myths come from? The stories of "things, or as Cayce referred to them, were used mostly as slaves in Atlantis, but there were those who wanted to make those being whole again and created temples of healing.

The problem with Atlantis was that most did not count love as their most important value in life. They were advanced scientifically but not spiritually. They understood crystals and the power of the mind, and their technology reached everywhere. The megalithic structures and pyramids throughout the world echo their technology. They understood mind control, and we are using it today to control humans.

Today, scientists alter genes and clone animals, but there is more taking place in laboratories that would shock you. Today scientists are creating the perfect soldier, a killing machine, half-human, and half AI, like the 1984 movie *Terminator*.

There was the Law of One, those spiritually advanced, and there were the Sons of Belial. The Sons of Belial sought material things for self-aggrandizement and indulgences without any consideration for the Freedom of Choice or decisions. In other words, they wanted to take away all democracy and freedom.

The Sons of Belial were greedy and wanted to control the entire planet and used the mighty Crystal's energy against their enemies. Some have compared the Crystal to a laser or nuclear-powered weapon, but it also harnessed energy for flying machines, submarines, and other advanced sciences.

Also, unlike Plato's description, Cayce's Atlantis was imperfect and like most civilizations, it was vulnerable to corruption and abuse of power. Cayce's readings blamed Atlantis' fall and the eventual destruction on greed, power, and the misuse of sciences to control the people, as we are seeing today. If we don't stop the insanity, these misuses will eventually bring us down, and like what happened to Atlantis, we might end up like the survivors that retrogressed to Mesolithic barbarism. Look at what is happening in America with increased violence and crime in the major cities since most cities defunded the police.

Writer and philosopher George Santayana said, "those who cannot remember the past are condemned to repeat it." How true! A large percentage of our young people haven't studied history, and they certainly don't know about Atlantis, not consciously. They have no idea that socialism is really communism. They demand that statues from our U.S. history should be torn down, names removed considered racist, and everything pertaining to the Civil War where soldiers fought and died to free black slaves from 1861 to 1865, one hundred fifty-seven years ago. They want history erased. It's not that we should dwell on the horrors of war, but why wars were fought for freedom, liberty, and justice for all.

A new civil disobedience is stirring worldwide among the young if their energy was used creatively and peacefully. Becoming cannon fodder is not the way to do it. That is their lesson to heal the Earth and humanity.

Has looting expensive items from stores helped them? You can't take physical items with you when you pass over to the spirit side. Their anger, hate, and violence send waves of negativity around the world. If they turned their hate to love, anger to calm, and violence to peace, the wave would travel around the world like a gentle breeze influencing others. Young people have a great responsibility, and I'm not talking about one particular race, religion, or sex. It encompasses all humans. As energy radiates and accelerates, billions of people will awaken from their slumber as we honor all lives and all life. We are all part of God but have failed to honor the God-consciousness and see the beauty in each soul on this planet.

Atlantis disappeared, but it wasn't erased from our DNA and our subconscious. Humans today recall how Atlantis, their home began crumbling as numbers relocated throughout the world bringing their technology of levitation used to move huge rock structures, which modern technology has not been able to duplicate monolithic stone structures like the Great Pyramid of Giza, Egypt.

Evidence of Atlantis

Before the end of the last ice age 12,000 years ago, the ocean levels were at least 300 feet below their current levels. Edgar Cayce referred to Bimini in the Caribbean as one of the mountaintops of ancient Atlantis. Although it would not be considered a mountain now, 12,000 years ago it was one of the highest points on the vast land formation in the region. Bimini and Andros Island, 100 miles to the East of Bimini, were part of the same island called "Poseidia" that sunk in 10,000 B.C., covered in the depth of the ocean, where records of Atlantis exist identical to the records in the Hall of Records hidden beneath the Sphinx on the Giza Plateau of Egypt.

In March 2020, Dr. Anthony Fauci told Mark Zuckerberg in an interview, *"This would not be the first time if it happened, that a vaccine that looked good in initial safety actually made people worse."*

CHAPTER THREE

COVID – MASS PSYCHOSIS

Here's a brief lesson in history and how it repeats to see where COVID is headed. Between 1918 and 1920, it is estimated that 50 million people worldwide, perhaps more, died of the Spanish Flu. It was one of the deadliest global pandemics since the Black Death or the bubonic plague that killed 75 to 200 million in Eurasia and North Africa from 1346 to 1351. The Spanish Flu struck down the young and healthy, often within days of exhibiting the first symptoms. The Spanish Flu was so virulent it put an end to World War I, killing more soldiers than the virus.

What's interesting is that the 1918 flu never went away, according to infectious disease experts. After infecting an estimated 500 million people worldwide between 1918 and some say into 1920, the H1N1 strain caused the Spanish Flu to recede into the background and has become the regular seasonal flu we see today.

Every so often, direct strains of the 1918 flu combined with the bird flu or swine flu to create powerful new strains. This happened in 1957, 1968, and 2009. Those flu outbreaks were part of the original 1918 virus that killed additional millions.

Jeffrey Taubenberg was part of the scientific team that first isolated and sequenced the genome of the 1918 flu virus in the late 1990s. The process involved extracting viral RNA from autopsied lung samples taken from American soldiers who died from the Spanish Fu in 1918, plus a diseased lung preserved in the Alaskan permafrost for nearly 100 years.

Taubenberger is now chief of the Viral Pathogenesis and Evolution Section at the National Institutes of Health (NIH). The genetic analyses of the 1918 flu indicated that it started as avian flu, a completely new viral strain when it made the leap to humans before 1918. Lab tests of the reconstructed 1918 virus show that in its original form, the virus's novel encoded proteins made it 100 times more lethal in mice than today's seasonal flu, which explains why it was such a deadly virus to humans.

The 1918 pandemic hit in three waves over 12-months. It first appeared in the spring of 1918 in North America and Europe mostly in the trenches of World War I. Reemerging in its deadliest form in the fall of 1918, killing tens of millions of humans globally from September through November. The final wave swept across Australia, the United States, and Europe in the late winter and spring of 1919.

Your existence today is because of your strong ancestors who had either strong antibodies to fight the Spanish Flu or somehow avoided it. Since the entire world was exposed to the virus and had therefore developed a natural immunity against it, the 1918 strain began to mutate and evolve in a process called "antigenic drift."

Slightly altered versions of the 1918 flu reemerged in the winters of 1919-1920 and 1920-1921, but they were far less deadly and are nearly impossible to differentiate from the seasonal flu today. Thankfully, the 1918 Spanish flu lost its virulence by the early 1920s.

History usually repeats itself, and we are already seeing the latest variant called Omicron has weakened compared to the original COVID-19 in 2020. People are still heading to the hospitals but surviving. Those who have died are usually obese, elderly, and those with compromised health issues.

I foresee that in the next two years, COVID will become another seasonal flu. People still died of the common flu, but not like the spread of COVID-19 in 2020 where hundreds of thousands died. There is hope for the future!

HOW COVID-19 BEGAN

Covid-19 reared its ugly head in mid-2019, and maybe earlier, according to some scientists. It was discovered that Dr. Anthony Fauci was involved with funding "Gain of Function" experiments at the Wuhan Laboratory as early as 2015. Gain-of-function is when an organism develops new abilities (or functions). This occurs in nature, or it can be achieved in a lab, when scientists modify the genetic code of place organisms in different environments, to change them in some way.

I predicted that COVID was not an accident release from the Wuhan laboratory as we have been told repeatedly. Again, mass hypnosis to make you believe their words. It was planned to be the culling of humanity for their world domination.

Dr. Anthony Fauci, an adviser to President Biden, director of the US National Institute of Allergy and Infectious Diseases (NIAID), part of the U.S. government's National Institutes of Health (NIH) gave money to an organization that collaborated with the Wuhan Institute of Virology. That organization—the US-based EcoHealth Alliance was awarded a grant in 2014 to look into the possibility of corona viruses from bats. EcoHealth received $3.7 million from the NIH, $600,000 of which was given to the Wuhan Institute of Virology.

Why was the US involved with any kind of virus funding, with China if it wasn't for a bioweapon?

In May, Dr. Fauci stated that the NIH "has not ever and does not now fund gain-of-function research in the Wuhan Institute of Virology." Senator Rand Paul asked Dr. Fauci if he wanted to retract that statement, saying, "As you are aware it is a crime to lie to Congress."

Fauci did not retract his words, but Senator Rand Paul believes the research did qualify as "gain-of-function" research and referred to two academic papers by the Chinese Institute, one from 2015 (written together with the University of North Carolina) and another from 2017. In 2019, its project was renewed for another five years but then pulled by President

Trump's administration in April 2020 following the outbreak of the coronavirus pandemic.

Dr. Fauci will go down in history as an evil man who was responsible for the deaths of millions of humans.

Professor Richard Ebright of Rutgers University told the BBC that the research in both papers showed that new viruses (that did not already exist naturally) were created, and these "risked creating new potential pathogens" that were more infectious. "The research in both papers was gain-of-function research," he stated.

As soon as the world began to get news of COVID-19 spreading quickly around the world by December 2019, I knew it had been released from a laboratory on purpose to decimate the world's population. 2022 is the year there will be greater control on the public and more of our freedom taken away. It was all planned years ago, but we were sleeping while they were planning their moves on humanity. In my *2020 Looking into the Future* book, I predicted that COVID-19 would never disappear. But like all viruses, it will mutate until it becomes a mild flu bug. Already the new variant Omicron is showing how mild it is, but more contagious.

Remember when Dr. Fauci reassured us that a face mask was not necessary. A few months later he changed his mind as he has done since 2020, and suggested mask mandates. He even went so far as to suggest two masks be worn. Even Biden and Nancy Pelosi said there would never be mask mandates or vaccine mandates. Of course, they lied, something they are fond of doing to us.

I watched a YouTube video by Dr. Robert Malone, a medical doctor and infectious disease researcher in the United States, and was awed by how right he is about the events taking place everywhere globally. Instead of giving his words verbatim, I will condense his words and meaning.

Dr. Malone referred to Mattias Desmet, a psychologist, and a statistician at the University of Ghent in Belgium. He's an impressive speaker and people like Robert Kennedy Jr. have met with him and spoken about his theories as many of Dr. Malone's peers.

Desmet has a theory he calls "Mass Formation Psychosis" Mass Formation is crowd psychosis, which is like hypnosis. This is what happened to the German people during World War II. If you lived in Europe or had a relative who survived the holocaust or lived behind the Soviet Union Curtain, in Eastern Europe, you'd understand what was happening during that time. How could the German people who were highly educated, very liberal in the classic sense, go crazy and do what they did to the Jews?

They were mind-controlled in the simplest sense.

Remember in 2019, the precursors for mass formation psychosis began in the population with COVID-19. People had become disconnected from everyone and everything except their cell phones and social media. There are no social bonds and great fragmentation in our communities—everyone fighting, disagreeing, angry, and hurtful. No one today feels connected. Our world is chaotic and overwhelming. Things don't make sense and there's a dire feeling of life-ending as we know it—that Armageddon has arrived.

Clearly, nothing makes sense.

Dr. Malone said that his wife experiences great psychological pain all the time. She wakes up in the middle of the night, suddenly alerted to something that she's been dreaming about. According to studies since 2020, more people have increased high blood pressure, especially women.

Think about what happened when the virus broke out. The world is obsessed with the virus. Suddenly every software person in the world was an expert on molecular virology and epidemiology. Dr. Malone had to deal with them. Everyone became obsessive experts spending all their time on the media, trying to figure out what was going on because it didn't make sense.

When these conditions happen and then the entire population gets focused on one thing, it forms something akin to mass hypnosis, where all they can think about. They are obsessed with that one thing. This is what happens with hypnosis (mind control).

If you can hypnotize someone and get them to focus on just one tiny thing before surgery, they won't feel any pain. This is a fundamental phenomenon of the human mind, the ability to become hypnotized by focusing all your attention on one thing. Once that happens, people lose their ability to have rational thought and judgment.

Even if you weren't obsessed, you had all this fear coming at you since 2020, on every news channel. Was this intentional?

There are a lot of signs that there was an intentional component. But we're sitting in a situation in which we have be actively managed psychologically by some entity that has financial benefit or power to gain from doing this. This gets to the point about Global Totalitarianism.

But regarding mass formation psychosis, once this happens there are two key things everybody gets focused on. They have this fusion of discontent. The focus is on one thing, and then our leaders step in to seize the moment and the population can see no evil, hear no evil, and that leader can speak no evil. And those leaders can say anything. It does not have to be true, and the crowd will believe it. Furthermore, with this kind of process mass formation psychosis that happened in 1930s Germany, we've seen in other situations—outside dissenters, anybody who says something contrary to the narrative must be attacked. They must have a common enemy.

This is well described in George Orwell's *1984* book, where there was a constant threat of the Eurasian Forces. They were nebulous. One never really knew where they were or if they were going to attack but there were always used to drive fear in the crowd.

So, this crowd now that's formed has central leaders that are lying to them all the time, like Dr. Tony Fauci. And as you see there's a narrow world in which those people have been hypnotized in this way. You can tell them until you're blue in the face what the data says, what the facts are, you can show them video clips of Tony Fauci lying. It doesn't matter.

Dr. Malone was in Tampa, Florida recently and a physician was asking questions and came up to him in the line broken-hearted. She has many other physicians and medical professionals in her family, and she's disaffected from all of them. And she said, "It doesn't matter how much information I provide to them, how many papers I provide to them, and what data I provide them, they can't hear it."

And that's true, they literally can't believe it because they are hypnotized.

This has happened all over the world. It's been actively promoted. It is the consequences of all this censorship and propaganda that we've seen subjected to and when it seems to you that the rest of the world has gone made, the truth is, they have.

The question is what can we do about it? So, he spoke to Mattias about this, about where he sees this going. And it's really a bit grim. He thinks that this mass psychosis has developed to a point where global totalitarianism is unavoidable.

We are seeing countries locking down their citizens, demanding "You will be vaccinated." Already Australia and Canada have become Marxist countries with dictator leaders. That flies in the face of data that shows that vaccinations won't stop the spread of the virus (maybe for a short time). They are talking about all kinds of mandates, and this includes very young children, which is harmful to them.

I foresee the virus mutating that it will be nothing more than the common cold and slight flu virus. Of course, people will still get deathly ill from the flu virus as they have for years. Omicron is waning now and by the end of 2022, it will be mostly gone. There will be new variants of COVID, but mostly innocuous. However, the fear mongers like Dr. Fauci, some Left Democrats, and the controlled media, will continue to tell us how bad things are going to get, and Biden will keep repeating it's the "unvaccinated" that are to blame for the spread of the virus. It's been proven that vaccinated people are more prone to get COVID or the variants with a breakthrough because the vaccines don't last that long. No matter how many vaccines you get, it won't help, and if it hasn't caused side effects already, it will. Fauci is already talking about another booster.

By 2023, we should be getting back to normal, including schools, if those who control us allow it. Although there will be more variants.

Many doctors, in the beginning, suggested therapeutics, including cheap generic drugs. Ivermectin is inexpensive but everyone in the media has branded it a horse medicine, yet I know for a fact people are leaving their death beds in hospitals after taking it. The pharmaceutical companies don't want you to have something inexpensive that can cure you of COVID, they want you to keep using their vaccines that harm you and don't last.

Trump's Operation Warp Speed project to develop vaccinations was ridiculed. Candidates Kamala Harris and Joe Biden talked down the safety of impending inoculations, but once in power they changed their insidious rhetoric to call people, "anti-vaxxers." Then like a child playing "opposite day" they claimed credit for the initial success of Trump's vaccinations.

It has been shown that Viagra has brought COVID patients out of their coma and can help Alzheimer's patients. An analysis of a large insurance-record database of more than seven million Americans has found that Viagra may reduce the risk of Alzheimer's dementia by almost 70 percent.

What can we do? First of all, honor your body. Get healthy and lose weight. Stop eating toxic and processed foods at fast-food restaurants. Start cooking healthy food you prepare. Too many women can't cook. People have become obese, and they are part of the huge numbers of people dying in hospitals from COVID. Some obese parents have children as young as three that are already so obese that they can hardly walk. That's criminal!

Next, we can stop the fear of the virus by not listening to major news that repeats that unvaccinated are racist and other berating rhetoric. That's pure mind control. We can break through to people if we help them to understand that what we're seeing is a coordinated global focus on deploying a global totalitarian solution. Totalitarianism is a bigger boogeyman than the virus is by far. Losing control to Bill Gates and the World Economic Forum is a bigger threat than SAR COV2 is for you or your children by far.

Note: some people believe they should intentionally get COVID to become immune. That's crazy!

Transforming fear
Dr. Jason Liu, a medical doctor, professor, and founder of the Mind-Body Institute of California understands why people have again become afraid to venture out to large gatherings as news about COVID-19 seems to be around every corner. As a doctor of holistic medicine, Liu looks at the whole person when it comes to health. Right now, people's immune systems are being attacked by the virus on three fronts.

"Right now, people have fear—that's the key," he said.

The pandemic has led to plummeting mental health and the rates of depression and anxiety have risen sharply, as well as suicides. At the most basic level, fear triggers our fight-or-flight response and the cascade of hormones and physiological changes that come with it. While this state is good for reacting to an immediate threat, it takes a significant toll on our well-being.

Music for healing

Beyond the healing power of the arts in general, Liu pointed out that the performance of Shen Yun's music blends ancient Chinese musical principles with the sound of the full classical orchestral that audiences are most familiar with. The ancient Chinese also believed that music had the power to heal. The Chinese characters for "music" are the root of Chinese characters for "medicine." The music system is pentatonic, based on five tones, which are attuned to the body's five main internal organs and the five elements of the exterior world.

This was common knowledge in traditional Chinese culture before communism. For 5,000 years, Chinese culture was believed to be divinely inspired, and the deeply spiritual civilization was centered around the idea of harmony between heaven, earth, and humankind. In 1949, the Communist Party, atheist, and anti-China in nature took power and undertook systematic and often gruesome campaigns to change the character of the nation.

Liu says, "We need to go back to our spiritual roots. Deeply connect with divine power, connect with God and the universe. Shen Yun uses historical stories and the power of music and dance to connect everyone with the original life source. People are ready for this. No matter what kind of religion you have, Christian or Buddhist, or qigong meditator, or yoga practitioners, there's a lot of spiritual practices still for those who understand it.

Source: Jan. 19-25, 2022, Epoch Times by Catherine Yang.

Betsey Lewis

CHAPTER 4

THE NEW RELIGION

Young people are embracing two new religions—Satanism and None. In the past several years the cancel culture decided that statues both religious and secular must be unceremoniously toppled—like Lenin after the fall of communism.

The rise of the Nones as they are now called have arrived in our world, the younger unaffiliated Americans who are growing in numbers. They don't have any religious beliefs and identify themselves as "None." They are mostly agnostic or atheists among generations or those who say their religion is "nothing in particular" and racial and ethnic groups. If they were a religion, they'd be the largest religious group in the United States, according to Elizabeth Drescher, an adjunct professor at Santa Clara University who wrote a book about the spiritual lives of the Nones.

Religious "nones" —a nickname used to refer to people who self-identify as atheists or agnostics, as well as those who say their religion is "nothing in particular" now make up roughly 23% of the U.S. adult population. This is a stark increase from 2007, the last time a similar pew research study was conducted when 16% of Americans were "nones." During this same period, Christians have fallen from 78% to 71%. Overall, religiously unaffiliated people are more concentrated among young adults than other age groups—35% of millennials (those born 1981-1996) are "nones." In addition, the unaffiliated people as a whole are getting even younger.

At the same time, even older generations have grown somewhat more unaffiliated in recent years. For example, 14% of Baby Boomers were unaffiliated in 2007, and 17% now identify as "nones." That's startling. "Nones" have made more gains through religious switching than any other group analyzed in the study." Only about 9% of U.S. adults say they were raised without a religious affiliation, and among this group, roughly half say that they now identify with a religion (most often Christianity). But nearly one-in-five Americans (18%) have moved in the other direction, saying that they were raised as Christians or members of another faith but that they now have no religious affiliation. That means more than four people have become "nones" for every person who has left the ranks of the unaffiliated.

"Nones" are more heavily concentrated among men than women. But the growth of the unaffiliated has not been limited to certain demographic categories; a rise in the share of unaffiliated has been seen across a variety of racial and ethnic groups, among people with different levels of education and income, among immigrants and the native-born, and throughout all major regions of the country.

Not only are the "nones" growing, but how they describe themselves is changing. Self-declared atheists or agnostics still make up a minority of all religious "nones." But both atheists and agnostics are growing as a share of all religiously unaffiliated people. Nearly two-thirds of atheists and agnostics are men, and the group also tends to be whiter and more highly educated than the general population.

Indeed, about 7% of U.S. adults say their religion is "nothing in particular" but also say that religion is "very" or "somewhat" important in their lives, despite their lack of a formal affiliation. This group is more racially and ethnically diverse than other "nones"; only 53% are non-Hispanic whites (compared with 66% of the public).

Some would say these young people are ripe for a charismatic leader to lead them to a new evil religion and some believe the Antichrist will be the one to lead them astray.

Does the name Moloch sound familiar? If you watched the Fox television series *Sleepy Hollow* (2013-2017) you will recall a demon named Moloch who returned to take over the world, but Ichabod Crane returned to the present day from the year 1781 to destroy Moloch and other demons from entering the world.

Two years ago, the Vatican approved the erection of a statue depicting the horned demon god Moloch at the coliseum in Rome. The site is known as a sacred site dedicated to Christian martyrs, and that's bizarre.

Demon Moloch erected near the Vatican

Talk show host Clyde Lewis wrote this in his monologue for Ground Zero on December 16, 2021: The presence of the statue at the Colosseum raised predictable concerns among the Christian faithful, who referred to it as a demon god at a holy site. Moloch is attested to in the Torah numerous times and appears to be associated with war and child sacrifice. Leviticus 18:21 mentions him: "And thou shalt not let any of thy seed pass through the fire to Molech."

According to Arthur Nobel and the European Institute of Protestant Studies, secret mystery school imagery and Catholic influenced Iconography is endemic in Europe and has been enthusiastically embraced by the European Union Parliament. He claims that it has startling similarities to the prophecies of Daniel Chapter 2 and Revelation Chapter 17 where a latter-day political union which, in its final form, will consist of ten nations or groups of nations dominated by the Antichrist and getting its power from the nation with seven hills (Rome) and being ruled by the Antichrist born of the Whore of Babylon.

The imagery associated with the European Union is strangely apocalyptic. The Euro coin blatantly has engraved on it a woman riding a beast. The E.U. parliament building appears to represent the unfinished tower of Babel. In front of the building are sculptures of a harlot riding the horned beast. Inside there are also tapestries depicting the same image.

European Parliament, Strasbourg, France   *Tower of Babel*, by Breugel (c. 1563)

Stranger yet, there are 679 seats in an auditorium where the fifth Parliament meets in the Tower building –While these seats are allocated to Members; one seat remains unoccupied. The number of that seat is 666. The seat has been set aside for the Antichrist.

The first president of the United Nations General Assembly, Paul-Henri Spaak, who was also the prime minister of Belgium and one of the early planners of the European Union as well as secretary-general of NATO, affirmed that they are awaiting the arrival of a savior when he stated, "We do not want another committee, we have too many already. What we want is a man of sufficient stature to hold the allegiance of all the people of the world and to lift us up out of the economic morass into which we are sinking. Send us such a man, and whether he be God or devil, we will receive him."

In 2016, Queen Elizabeth of England approved the erection of a statue of the Mesopotamian demon Pazuzu on one of her Crown Estate buildings at the mall in London.

This confirms that these people have a relationship with Satan.

The Precious New Children

Special children are being born at this time, but they are going to have a difficult time with the dark agendas happening on Earth. They are confused and depressed and not able to be taught higher learning. They will suffer greatly with fear of the future. Horrible vaccine mandates have been forced on them when most children have a natural immunity to COVID. They have been forced to wear masks in school rooms which harm their breathing and some schools have forced them to exercise with masks. This is so wrong!

Future generations need to learn about the natural world and arcane wisdom from the ancients and indigenous people that there are signs in nature that warn us, nature can heal us naturally, and that everything exists for a reason. Everything on Earth has a symbiotic relationship with other lifeforms. Life is balanced until humans start interfering. It's the creativity that sets them free.

Children around the world are abused both mentally and sexually, and that sets them on a road to abusing others. If the rioters, mostly millennials, who have rioted in major cities, looted and burned businesses, and killed others, have no respect for life that falls on the parents. How can the parents of these hoodlums teach them about respect when they are walking drugged zombies?

When the universe functions in a harmonic way, without tyranny, one civilization is free to exchange information with another.

My friend and mentor, Corbin Harney, spiritual leader of the Western Shoshone Nation, was worried about the young people coming into the world. He said, "If we had followed the spiritual way of life, we would never have been doing what we're doing today because the spiritual way of life is to take care of what we've got, so that we can have a cleaner life and continue to live on. Today, we're beginning to realize that we have to connect with the spirits out there for us to continue."

Corbin admonished the younger people harming their bodies. "Our people have been hiding a lot of lies, alcohol, and marijuana smoke. When people go that way, their mind disappears—it's not there anymore. If we continue to do that, where are we going to be? Where are all the youngsters going to be within another ten to twenty years, if that's the kind of life we have to live? We know these things are poison. We, humans, are the only beings who don't seem to understand how poisonous these things are. The animals, the birds, they understand. We continue on and on, taking poison until we ruin our life or take our own life. "

Corbin passed in 2007, and he would have been deeply saddened by how marijuana and stronger drugs like heroin and Fentanyl are plentiful in today's world. He wondered how youngsters would lead us in the future.

Corbin said we are connected to everything, even though we might not realize it. He said, "we have to remember that all living things on this Earth have spirits. Always offer something to what you get off the land. Bless what you get from Mother Earth. Bless the water. Talk to it, keep it alive, keep it moving. Keep the Spirit in the water moving. If you talk to it and bless it, it really keeps the water happy, and gives it strength."

Corbin cautioned young people, "Once we lose that connection between the Spirit world and us, then who can we rely on?"

CHAPTER 5

SATANISM

Most of the awakened people sense *"something wicked this way comes,"* a line taken from Act IV of William Shakespeare's Macbeth.

On October 29, 2021, President Biden visited Pope Francis in Rome, and according to Biden the Pope told him that he was a "good Catholic and should continue receiving communion. But how can Biden be a "good Catholic" when he supports abortion, and the Catholic Church condones it.

The revelation of the Pope's words to Biden came after American bishops moved forward with a plan that tried to permit individual bishops to deny communion to politicians who support abortion rights, setting up a potential public rebuke of Biden along with other prominent Catholic Democrats, such as House Speaker Nancy Pelosi.

In April of 2013, my book, *Mystic Revelations of Thirteen* was published about the number 13 in numerology is a power number used by the Illuminati, and also by Pope Francis. When a number repeats numerous times, it goes beyond coincidence.

Perhaps this will convince you that many of our leaders are steeped in mysticism and even satanism. On March 13, 2013, a date which totals 13, I was invited to be a guest on *Ground Zero Radio Show* with host Clyde Lewis to discuss the synchronicities of the number 13, but little did I know that the show was about to change in an unforeseen way. My intuition said something big would happen that day, and it did!

Pope Benedict XVI stunned the world by announcing his resignation on February 28, 2013. The Cardinals quickly gathered in Rome and on March 13, 2013, Cardinal Jorge Mario Bergoglio of Argentina was elected the new pope by the Cardinals gathered in Rome. Bergoglio decided on the papal name of Pope Francis I in honor of Saint Francis of Assisi, the 13th-century friar, and preacher known for his humility toward nature, animals, and the poor.

Jorge Mario Bergoglio now Pope Francis became the first Jesuit pope, turning 76-years-old on December 17, 2012. Again, his age of 76 totaled the number 13.

In 1967 Bergoglio finished his theological studies and was ordained to the priesthood on December 13, 1969, by Archbishop Ramòn José Castellano. He attended the Facultades de Filosofía y Teología de San Miguel (Philosophical and Theological Faculty of San Miguel). Father Bergoglio completed his final stage of spiritual formation as a Jesuit, tertianship, at Alcalá de Henares, Spain, and took his perpetual vows in the Society of Jesus on April 22, 1973 (22 is a sacred Illuminati number). He was named Provincial Superior of the Society of Jesus in Argentina on July 31, 1973, and served until 1979. Thirty-one reversed is 13.

On June 4, 1997, Bergoglio was appointed Coadjutor Archbishop of Buenos Aires with the right of automatic succession. His episcopal motto was *Miserando atque eligendo* drawn from Bede's homily on Matthew 9:9-13. Again, the number 13.

The Irish Saint Malachy had a list of 112 (1+12 = 13) short Latin couplets which are said to describe each of the Roman Catholic popes along with a few anti-popes beginning with Pope Celestine II, elected in 1143 and concluding with Pope Benedict XVI's successor, a pope described in the prophecy as "Peter the Roman", whose pontificate will end in the destruction of the city of Rome (perhaps an earthquake).

Here's where things get even stranger. Cardinal Jose Mario Bergoglio, an Italian (Roman) took the name Francis from Francis of Assisi, the 13th century Italian Saint, who was born Giovanni di Pietro di Bernardone. Pietro is Italian for "Peter." Could it be he decided on the name Francis to throw conspiracy theorists off that he is "Petrus Romanus," the fulfillment of the old Malachy prophecy? Sounds farfetched but nothing surprises me anymore.

Former Bishop Gerard Bouffard of Guatemala said the Vatican is "the real spiritual controller" of the Illuminati and New World Order. Jesuits have been linked to mysticism and some say to the secret occult society, The Illuminati. The Illuminati is the name given to a small group of noble and non-noble families in the 18th Century that assisted the Jesuit Order in their plans to exact revenge on the Catholic Church for their disbandment in July 1773 by Pope Clement XIV and the order *Dominus ac Redemptor.*

It is believed the Illuminati families were instrumental in assisting the Jesuits in stealing both the gold reserves of the Catholic Church and the French State through the promotion of the French Revolution and then Napoleon. Some say it is a certainty that the Jesuits obtained many extremely important and incriminating documents from the Vatican Secret Archives during the capture of Rome by the forces of Napoleon Bonaparte in 1796.

Latin America's first pope was clouded by lingering concerns about the role of the church and its new head during Argentina's brutal military dictatorship. The Catholic church and Pope Francis have been accused of a complicit silence and worse during the "dirty war" of murders and abductions carried out by the junta that ruled Argentina from 1976 to 1983. Although the evidence is sketchy and contested, documents were destroyed and many of those who were victims or perpetrators have died in the years that followed. It was a dangerous time to speak out and risk being labeled subversive. But many, including priests and bishops, did speak out and subsequently disappeared. Those who stayed silent have subsequently had to live with their consciences and sometimes the risk of a trial.

Satanism involves sexual abuse. Many leaders, people you look up to, particularly in the fields of politics, religion, and education that seem dedicated to children are in reality a massive covert organization of pedophiles who use children for sex. This happens because it is passed on from generation to generation. This is one of the darkest secrets of the Family of Dark. The houses of the rich are riddled with this secret: sex with family members, sex for ritual abuse, sex for calling-in darkness, and the dark Goddess, where no vibration of love exists, only a vibration of power.

It's no secret that numbers of priests in the United States and worldwide have been accused of abusing children and have never been punished for their crimes. This is one of the darkest secrets of the Family of Dark on Earth. The elite and rich (think about the men who were accused of participating with pedophile Jeffrey Epstein—former President Bill Clinton, Prince Andrew, Bill Gates, and God knows who else, but Epstein was murdered in jail before he could testify. He did not commit suicide. Even Donald Trump had a photograph taken with Epstein with his arm around a young girl. While he has minimized his relationship with Epstein in recent years, Trump's previous comments speak for themselves. "I've known Jeff for fifteen years. Terrific guy," Trump told New York Magazine in 2002. "He's a lot of fun to be with. It is even said that he likes beautiful women as much as I do, and many of them are on the younger side."

We don't know Donald Trump's involvement with Epstein, so we should not rush to judgment about whether or not he was involved with underaged girls. Trump has a huge ego, which has been his major problem with voters. He's too bombastic and that gets him in trouble. Many former presidents had mistresses, but did that make them horrible presidents? As the Bible says, *Let him who is without sin cast the first stone.*

Epstein was charged with sexually exploiting and abusing dozens of minor girls at his homes in New York City, Palm Beach, Florida, the US Virgin Islands, and other locations from 2002 to 2005. His US Virgin Islands home had an Egyptian temple on the grounds, and it has never been revealed what it was used for. Through my remote viewing, I can tell you that perverse satanic rituals were conducted inside the temple.

A contractor and engineer who spoke to *Insider* said the odd architectural detail had a medieval-era lock on the front door that was designed to keep people inside. A piano tuner who came to the Little St. James 70-acre private island claimed there's an entrance to an underground lair beneath the temple and it was built for an ancient evil deity. A monument to sexual predation.

Another conspiracy theory claimed the statues depicted in the temple represent a deity of the ancient Canaanite religion, whose adherents practiced child sacrifice: "It's actually an 'owl,' and it's the same as the great 'owl' at Bohemian Grove—the 'owl' is Moloch, the satanic entity that demands child sacrifice."

Back to Biden—Biden's daughter, Ashley Biden, claimed in her diary that her father asked her to take "not appropriate" showers with him as a child and she hinted at sexual abuse. Have you watched all the videos of Biden whispering into little girls' ears and playing with their hair?

You probably wonder why Jill Biden has never said anything to protect her children. Look at Hunter Biden who has been involved with sex trafficking and drugs, and their daughter Ashley. As they say, the apple doesn't fall far from the tree. Many women have sexually abusive fathers, and the mothers never said or did anything about it. Shocking! Usually, the mother was abused as well and will not speak up fearing injury or death.

Those who are destroying our democracy are devoid of love and do not realize it. Instead of pretending this darkness doesn't exist, our responsibility is to make this public. Our task of healing the planet will grow greater as the secrets of the world's ruling families and their dark occult practices are discovered.

These are your so-called "antichrists," that you have feared for ages, and never recognized them as ordinary people with power. They are like the Wizard of Oz hiding behind the curtain, at the controls, creating chaos and fear in our lives.

For years we have gone about our lives without looking beyond the walls, believing our leaders are benevolent people who will save us from ourselves. But we drink, eat societies poisons, and turn our children over to Big Brother, the mind-control World Management Team where one does not think but simply performs.

Many parents have now discovered their children are being taught things they had no idea about CRT (Critical Race Theory). They have been told that white people are racists or "white supremacists," which Biden had repeated in speeches. Yet, those who are yelling "white supremacists" are often white people—Caucasians.

Parents have tried to protest such teachings and have been either jailed or detained by police for disrupting School Board Meetings. Suddenly parents find they don't have a right to their child's education.

Angry protests will continue from people worldwide, and the energies will intensify to an outrageous state, energies that ask each of you to change. There will be shocks and scandals, and more freedoms taken away from you the like of which you have never seen. Ideally, you will wake up and see that what is happening in one country is happening everywhere, and it will seem like it was instantaneous. That's because it was planned long ago, while most of us slept.

Most of us live in a bubble, listening to the mainstream media and political Leftists tell us how we should live and how we should be obedient and get our COVID-19 shots, despite the side effects they try to hide from us. Biden has given us the mandates like a dictator, where we have no choice but to obey his commands or lose our jobs and be shunned by society.

Corruption in the United States among politicians and justices is ubiquitous. Not all, but most, and it's pervasive in our world.

Father Malachi on Satanism

Father Malachi Martin, born July 23, 1921, and died July 27, 1999, was an Irish Catholic priest and controversial author. Originally ordained as a Jesuit priest, he became a Professor of Paleontology at the Vatican's Pontifical Biblical Institute, and from 1958 he served as a theological adviser to Cardinal Augustin Bea during the preparations for the Second Vatican Council. Through the years he became disillusioned by reforms in the Church and renounced his vows in 1964, moving to New York City. His 17 novels and non-fiction books were often critical of the Catholic Church. He believed the Church should have disclosed the third secret of Fatima, Portugal as the Virgin Mary had requested. Two of his books, *The Scribal Character of The Dead Sea Scrolls,* 1958, and *Hostage to the Devil,* 1976, dealt with Satanism, demonic possession, and exorcism.

Father Malachi Martin's accusations

In *The Fatima Crusader* article, Father Malachi Martin, a former Jesuit priest, a scholar, a Vatican insider, and best-selling author, said, "Anybody who is acquainted with the state of affairs in the Vatican in the last 35 years is well aware that the prince of darkness has had and still has his surrogates in the court of Saint Peter in Rome."

From 1958 until 1964, Jesuit priest Malachi Martin served in Rome where he was a close associate of the renowned Jesuit Cardinal Augustin Bea and the Pope. Released afterward from his vows of poverty and obedience at his own request (but as a priest), Father Martin moved to New York and became a best-selling writer of fiction and non-fiction. He often made references to satanic rites held in Rome in his 1990 non-fiction best-seller, *The Keys of This Blood*, in which he wrote: "Most frighteningly for [Pope] John Paul [II], he had come up against the irremovable presence of a malign strength in his own Vatican and certain bishops' chanceries. It was what knowledgeable Churchmen called the 'superforce.' Rumors, always difficult to verify, tied its installation to the beginning of Pope Paul VI's reign in 1963. Indeed, Paul had alluded somberly to 'the smoke of Satan which has entered the Sanctuary'. . . an oblique reference to an enthronement ceremony by Satanists in the Vatican. Besides, the incidence of Satanic pedophilia—rites and practices— was already documented among certain bishops and priests as widely dispersed as Turin, in Italy, and South Carolina, in the United States.

The cultic acts of Satanic pedophilia are considered by professionals to be the culmination of the Fallen Archangel's rites."

Father Martin said, "Satanism is all around us. We deny it at our peril. I could point out places only minutes from here [New York City] where black masses are being celebrated. I know of cases of human sacrifice—the sacrifice of babies. I know the people who are doing these things."

Veronica Lueken's Visions

Veronica Lueken from Bayside, New York began to have visions of the Blessed Virgin Mary (BVM) and Jesus over 25 years starting in 1985.

Veronica: "Oh! Our Lady is also pointing over with a very angry look on Her face. And I see—oh, a terrible . . . oh, it's—oh, my goodness! I know what it is; I see . . . I know they're human beings, but they're wearing black garments and slit holes in their faces.

And the BVM said: "See, My child, the worship of the prince of evil. You are shocked, My child? Do not delude yourselves that this does not exist upon your earth now, the worship of Satan. Pagans! Pagans in the House of God! Pagans roaming your nations, leaders of your nations giving themselves to Satan!" June 15, 1974.

On May 18, 1977, the Blessed Virgin Mary told Veronica, "In the Eternal City of Rome, the forces of evil have gathered. Secretly in secret societies, and openly by brazen mankind shall come forth revolution."

The Murder of Pope John Paul I

The Blessed Virgin Mary's apparition, at Bayside, New York, stated that Satan had entered into "the highest realms of the hierarchy in Rome" and she would also explain some very dark secrets surrounding the death of Pope John Paul I, who suddenly died of a "heart attack" slightly over a month after the election. The Blessed Virgin Mary's message at Bayside New York affirmed, "Man has fallen very low, even (resorting) to murder." (October 6, 1978).

And on May 21, 1983, she said: "We will go back, my child, in history, a short history, and remember well what had happened in Rome to John, Pope John, whose reign lasted 33 days (note Illuminate master number 33). Oh, my child, it is history now, but it is placed in the book that lists the disasters in mankind. He received the horror and martyrdom by drinking from a glass. It was a champagne glass given to him by a now deceased member of the clergy and the Secretariat of the State."

Does that sound incredible? Consider this: a 1975 ruling from the Vatican ordered that no autopsy could be performed on a Pope. What did the Vatican have to fear from an autopsy? Our Lady's message pointed to foul play. Also, there is a best-selling book, *In God's Name: An Investigation into the Murder of Pope John Paul I,* by David Yallop, that alleges Pope John Paul I was murdered.

This is another hint of what the *real* Third Secret of Fatima might contain. "But, my children, as I said in the past, I repeat again, that Satan and his agents, the band of 666, has entered into the highest places of the hierarchy; and therefore he has captured some of Our formerly noble hierarchy to do his bidding."- *Our Lady of the Roses, June 1, 1978*

On October 2, 1974, the Blessed Virgin Mary gave this prophecy to Veronica, "A disaster of great magnitude is approaching your country! Have you prepared for this? There will be in your country a great quake. The earth shall tremble, the homes shall fall, and many shall be sent into oblivion! Many shall not be prepared and will be claimed by Satan! Pray, pray, My children! Send your Messages far and wide! A great disaster is approaching mankind! Your country will not escape this chastisement. Do not, my child, put this in the same measure as the Chastisement in the near future. This will be an additional warning to mankind!"

I suspect this disaster is Planet X's approach to Earth and how its magnetic pulls will cause the shift of Earth's poles or a massive solar flare hitting Earth in our future.

Jeffrey Epstein and his sex cult

Jeffrey Epstein roomed young teen women to become his sex slaves for himself, his girlfriend Ghislaine Maxwell, and powerful men like Prince Andrew, former President Bill Clinton, and possibly Bill Gates and others, including Donald Trump were photographed with him on several occasions. In one video Trump appeared to be laughing with Epstein observing women in the room. Perhaps a private joke. Many well-known men were taken to Epstein's Island in the Caribbean where God knows what took place.

A temple that looks like the headgear of an Egyptian Pharaoh, stands on the Island. Conspiracy theorists have suggested that the temple had an elevator that took them to a room where orgies took place, and other religious or satanic rituals took place involving women. Maxwell is probably the only one who can reveal what the Egyptian-looking building was used for.

Other investigators believe the building was only a study for Epstein to listen to music, read and do his business work. A grand piano was found inside the domed building. The island, known as Little St. James, was purchased by Epstein in 1998 and was raided by the FBI in 2019 while building a case against him concerning the alleged sex trafficking of minors.

In 2019, despite being a registered sex offender, locals say Epstein was still flying in underage girls, according to a Vanity Fair investigation. Epstein died in jail by suicide in 2019 under mysterious circumstances, but I had a vision of him being strangled. He was murdered. As they say, "Dead men tell no tales," and those who were involved with him were scared that he'd rat on them. Epstein was an international sex trafficker.

Currently, Ghislaine Maxwell's trial is taking place. Epstein's pilot David Rodgers testified on the who's who of powerful men—former Presidents Bill Clinton and Donald Trump. He said they had flown on Epstein's private plane, Lolita Express on several occasions. He was Epstein's private pilot for 28 years. He recalled renowned violinist Itzhak Perlman flew to Michigan with Epstein for the Interlochen Center for the Arts summer camp. He said he remembered Prince Andrew, Maine Sen. George Mitchell, Ohio Sen. John Glenn, and actor Kevin Spacey, known to be gay, on flights. He also claimed he'd fly Epstein to Columbus, Ohio where Epstein had property to see billionaire businessman Lex Wexner.

Maxwell faces more than 70 years in prison if convicted on all counts of sex trafficking, sex trafficking conspiracy, and charges related to facilitating the travel of minors for sexual acts as young as 14-year-old. She may end up dead like Epstein, and it won't be from suicide.

MK-Ultra experiments and satanism
On August 3rd, 1977, the 95th U.S. Congress opened hearings into the reported abuses concerning the CIA's TOP SECRET mind control research program code named MK-Ultra. On February 8th, 1988, a top-level MK-Ultra victim, Cathy O'Brien, was covertly rescued from her mind control enslavement by Intelligence insider Mark Phillips, now deceased. Their seven-year pursuit of Justice was stopped for reasons of national security.

Trance Formation of America exposed the truth behind this covert government program and its ultimate goal: *psychological control of a nation.* The book is the first documented autobiography of a victim of government mind control.

In Cathy and Mark's book, *Trance Formation of America*, she traced her path from child pornography and recruitment into the program to serving as a top-level intelligence agent and

White House sex slave to the Clinton's, former President George H.W. Bush, and Dick Cheney. It's a definitive eye-witness account of government corruption that implicates some of the most prominent figures in U.S. politics.

In some of the events, Cathy described sexual encounters where she had to run in a rural field while she was hunted like an animal. The sexual and mind control abuse of Cathy as a young child and young woman was similar to what military mind control involved in breaking down an enemy's power.

There is evil on this planet and there are those followers of Satan involved in the dark arts that pull in dark entities during their ceremonies.

In 2021, President Biden met with Pope Francis, and Pope Francis said that he is a good Catholic despite his belief in abortion. The Roman Catholic Church has consistently condemned abortion—the direct and purposeful taking of the life of the unborn child. Yet, how could Pope Francis say that about Biden if Pope Francis was truly the Pope he portrays to the world. He's a wolf in sheep's clothing doing dark work as I indicated earlier.

The Catholic Church for hundreds of years has been involved in dark dealings. In recent years, countless priests have been charged with sexual abuse of underaged children, only to have their hands slapped and nothing more. The former pope Benedict XVI failed to act against four priests accused of child sexual abuse when he was archbishop of Munich, a German investigation has claimed.

Since the 1950s the French clergy sexually abused more than 200,000 children, mostly young boys, ages 10 to 13. The Catholic Church had turned a blind eye to the scourge of helpless children.

The truth is that churches have hidden their dark sexual sins from their flocks for a long time.

The Pleiadians and their message

From 1992 to 1999 Barbara Marciniak wrote a series of channeled books given to her by the Pleiadians. In her book, *Family of Light*, the Pleiadians said, "As we share the dark part of the story with you, such as the covert and perverted sexual practices of your rulers, it is not for us to name names. You will discover for yourself that in every country around the globe, those in the highest of positions have been put there because they are qualified by their perversions to hold powers over others. This has been a secret for eons, but today everyone is coming out of the closet, so to speak.

"Do not become frightened when your leaders fall. It is all designed so you can know the worst of family secrets: that parents sexually abuse their children from generation to generation because they do not know love. Love must prevail. You must clean your biological line, the ethers, and the astral plane because the new children wanting to be born will only be attracted by a frequency that guarantees they will be cherished. Without the cherishing of your children, you do not guarantee the continuity of humankind on Earth. This also requires that you respect and cherish the sexual act, for the quality of your couplings will determine the frequency in your energy field."

The Pleiadians continued, "The mind controllers and those who influence the weather and all aspects of your economy, religion, education, and medicine will be revealed because you are now ready to take charge and influence yourselves. Those responsible for your plight think they are so much better than you; however, their darkness creates endless difficulties for them.

"You must begin to heal these wounds. Your compassion and forgiveness must include an understanding of existence on a scale broader than any apparent singular 3-D events, a realization that these misuses of power are predominant throughout the pages of the book, *Earth*. The healing must be deep. In this process, you will find your power and ideally heal your wounded leaders, and wounded they are indeed. Some will self-heal; others will proclaim their shame and, once they have exposed their darkness, become great leaders. However, most will create their own destruction, and you will have to clear the astral planes of their polluted forms."

Interestingly, the Pleiadians talked about strange things in the sky. "Unusual sightings in the heavens will continue—streaks and balls of light, comets, mysterious fires in the skies, unusual lightning, and bizarre phenomena. We remind you once again that without the dark you would not see this play of light. The cosmic frequencies involve many layers of plans. The Creator is in everything, so is anything natural. Is it not all connected? Frequency control of your mind will become a paramount issue of concern on your planet: how you are given visions through television, computers, music, movies, and through invisible microwave transmissions that influence your thought patterns and your patterns of living. Mind control will be seen as the ultimate battle with darkness."

The Pleiadians warned of mind control, and said, "Uncovering the dark in all its awesome power will herald for you the power of the Gods. It will be one thing to face the perverse practices and mind control of your world leaders and to take a stand and demand integrity, yet at the same time want to destroy [them]. However, it will be quite another thing indeed for you to stand back—like the story of David before the giant Goliath—when you begin to understand the entities that these very wounded world leaders really present.

"We ask you, with the courage of your being, to call forth the darkness that is waiting to be healed. From a place of love and a place of courage, as Family of Light, we ask you to send out a call and say, 'Darkness, misuse of power, violation, and perversion of peoples and the Earth herself, it's time for you to reveal yourselves. And in the revealing, there will be healing. So come forward Dark that the world may know you, and then we may know the Light and all rejoice as one.

"This is a noble call and does not imply that the darkness will take over your life. You are calling for darkness and misuse of energy to be healed so that all humans can express their sexuality with love so that children are honored and given a rightful opportunity to initiate their own sexual explorations without having sex forced upon them through ritual rape and violation."

If you have not read Barbara Marciniak's work, I highly recommend *Earth: Pleiadian Keys to the Living Library, Brings of the Dawn: Teachings from the Pleiadians, and Family of Light*. This information, I believe, contains some of the most essential teachings for our times relating to the seen and unseen world around us and the multidimensional beings who co-exist with us.

The Anti-Christ by psychic Jeane Dixon

Jeane Dixon (January 5, 1904 – January 25, 1997) was one of the best-known Christian astrologers and mystic seers of the 20th century because of her syndicated newspaper astrology column, her well-known predictions, and best-selling biography. She foretold President John F. Kennedy's assassination and tried to warn him of the event, and she even named his alleged killer Oswald. She also warned the second Secretary-General of the United Nations, Dag Hammerskjöld, not to fly in the plane which crashed in September 1961. He was killed in the crash. On May 14, 1953, in an NBC telecast, Jeane said, "A silver ball will emerge from Russia, to travel in space!" Many critics laughed at such a notion, until four years later when Russia launched the Sputnik 1 space capsule into space!

She also predicted the assassinations of Mahatma Gandhi, Martin Luther King, and Robert Kennedy. One of Jeanne Dixon's prophecies, published in the 1970s, was fulfilled in part when Mehmed Aÿca shot Pope John Paul II on Wednesday, May 13, 1981:

"During this century one pope will suffer bodily harm. Another will be assassinated. The assassination will be the final blow to the office of the Holy See. This pope will be the same one who will be chosen in the not too distant future but whose election will not be approved by the Roman clergy. His influence, however, will be such that he will win out over the objections of his opponents. While this pope will be the last one ever to reign as singular head of the Church, the beginnings of this change will occur with one of his predecessors who will give far-reaching powers to his cardinals. These same cardinals will use their powers to replace him with one more to their liking."

Like the 14th-century prophet Nostradamus and St. John (Revelation 8: 8-12), Jeane Dixon had a vision that Earth will be struck by a comet, but her timing was either premature or wrong: *"I have seen a comet strike our Earth around the middle of the 1980s. Earthquakes and tidal waves will befall us as a result of the tremendous impact of this heavenly body in one of our great oceans..."*

Like several other prophets, Jeane Dixon had foreseen the advent of the Antichrist and the False Prophet: *"Satan is now coming into the open to seduce the world and we should be prepared for the inevitable events that are to follow. I have seen that the United States is to play a major role in this development... I have seen a government within a government develop in the US within the last few years... I see this government within a government being controlled and financed by a well-oiled political machine of one of our leading* political families [Bush family?]. With their eye on the White House, I see them discredit any man who occupies it without their approval, no matter how good his political programs may be.

"They will—through political intimidation, propaganda, and illegal sixth-column activities—make every effort to show the nation that only their man, the one who heads their machine, has the sole right to occupy the White House. Their campaign is going to cause great harm to our nation both here and abroad.

"I see this group succeed in taking over de facto control of the country. They will give rise to an upheaval in our social structure as never before seen. They will bring about increased social unrest and great discontent. Foreign subversive elements will—as they did in the 1960s—infiltrate the unruly factions and cause renewed fighting on the nation's campuses and in racial ghettos.

"All of the evil in the masses will be swept toward an unknown frenzy by this machine.

"I see a member of this machine ascend to power in New York City, enforcing new laws and regulations that will affect many households of that great metropolis. Obviously, the Rockefellers are indicated here.

"The social and religious chaos generated by this political machine throughout the United States will prepare the nation for the coming of the prophet of the Antichrist. This political unit of the East will be the tool of the serpent in delivering the masses to him.

"The False Prophet's domain shall be the intellectual seduction of mankind. It means a mixture of political, philosophical, and religious ideology that will throw the populations of the world into a deep crisis of faith in God... One of his first duties and responsibilities in readying the world for the advent of his master is to manipulate the available propaganda machines. With teaching and propaganda, the prophet will cause people not merely to accept the Antichrist but rather to desire him with positive enthusiasm to create the conditions of his coming and to participate in organizing the frightful and terrifying despotism of his World Empire.

"[The seemingly miraculous phenomena he will produce] will not be supernatural or preternatural events but rather *prodigies of science and human achievements but interpreted in such a way as to lead men away from God and toward the worship of the Antichrist...The prophet of the Antichrist and the Antichrist himself will be specific and identifiable persons!"*

Although Jeane had her psychic misses, she was amazingly accurate on several world predictions. She received a vision on February 5, 1962, that she believed was of utmost importance to the world. She wrote, *"A child born somewhere in the Middle East shortly before 7:00 A.M. (EST) on February 5, 1962, will revolutionize the world. Before the close of this century, he will bring together all mankind in one all-embracing faith. This will be the foundation of a new Christianity, with every sect and creed united through this man who will walk among the people to spread the wisdom of the almighty powers."*

Although she wasn't positive, she thought this was the day of his birth, as it was a significant date—the 66th day of the year as having great importance by mystics and astrologers. She saw the man plotting with his followers as early as the age of 19, a time when something important happened to him, around 1973. His impact would be felt by the world at age 29 or 30, in 1992.

Jeane also believed this man had actual ancient Egyptian lineage to the heretic Pharaoh Akhenaten and his Queen Nefertiti, and she felt that he had lived in the Arab world for a time. She believed that he would become a leader of Egypt (this hasn't happened yet). I found this prediction eerily fascinating because Pharaoh Akhenaten was called the heretic that turned the world from its former Egyptian gods to worship one god, Aten, in the form of the sun. Some believe that he wanted self-aggrandizement, but others say he started monotheism.

Akhenaten tried to bring about a departure to traditional religion, but it was a failure. After his death, traditional Egyptian religious practice was gradually restored. He was expunged from records by succeeding rulers and referred to as the enemy.

Although he had six daughters with Nefertiti, recent DNA tests showed that he fathered a son, Tutankhamen, with his biological sister.

Jeane felt that her vision of Akhenaten and Nefertiti presenting their modern son to the world as a fit and final heir to their rebel throne as the final Antichrist world ruler so often predicted in the Bible. Besides this, she also believed he would have infinite and Satanic wisdom, knowledge, and a hypnotic personality, that "all the world will wonder after him," as predicted in Revelation 13. Frighteningly, her vision portrayed this leader as charismatic where the youth of the world idolize him like a god.

At the end of her vision, Jeane saw him leading the followers to a place of decision and division where they could either follow him to the left or take the straight and narrow road to the right, away from him and righteousness. Many would see his true dark nature and leave him, climbing over difficult obstacles along the narrow path that led to the right.

As an astrologer, I used the date Jeane Dixon had given as the Antichrist's birthdate—February 5, 1962, 7:00 am EET, to cast an astrological chart, and used Alexandria, Egypt as his birthplace.

I was stunned at what I found. If this person does exist, their chart shows 7 planets in Aquarius—the sun, rising sign, the moon, Mercury, Venus, Mars, Jupiter, and Saturn, which is remarkable in itself. No matter where this person was born, he'd still have 7 planets in Aquarius but in different degrees. Uranus is in Leo, Neptune in Scorpio, Pluto in Virgo and his North Node in Leo. Having three Aquarius signs in the first house would give this person an enormous ego and power, and a need for fame and recognition. The other four Aquarius signs reside in the twelfth house; the house of the inner self, dreams, illusions, and mysticism/occult. He will be the great deceiver and have occult powers.

What would the Antichrist represent? First and foremost, he'd be against Christ and his teachings, and he'd have ancient occult knowledge. With seven planets in Aquarius, he'd view the world with a detached attitude and unconventional air.

Is there any person that has this birth date that is currently world-known? Not that we know of, but suppose this person knowing Jeane Dixon's famous prediction changed his birthdate to hide his true identity?

Some conspiracy theorists believe former President Barack Obama was the anti-Christ and some have suggested it was Donald Trump. If anyone comes close to being the antichrist, it's George Soros, born in 1930 to a Jewish family, he is a Hungarian-born American multi-billionaire investor and philanthropist. He believes in no borders in countries worldwide and he has openly claimed he is not spiritual and doesn't believe in God. He has donated to U.S. elections. He also backs the political fundraising group called Democracy Alliance for progressive causes and a stronger progressive infrastructure in America.

If such a person exists, he hasn't made himself known...not yet anyway.

CHAPTER 7

THE MOON AND MARS

In 2020, Elon Musk announced his dream to have Space X land humans on Mars by 2026. NASA plans to return astronauts to the Moon by 2024 with the Artemis Mission. Will these timelines be realized in such a short time?

Musk outlined the 2026 goal at the International Astronautical Congress in September 2016, and said, "I don't want to say that's when it will occur—there's a huge amount of risk."

China will send its astronauts to the Moon in 2023 or early 2024, and Musk's ambition to send astronauts to Mars will take place, but not without difficulties on the way to Mars. It will take an estimated seven months to get there with a good planetary alignment.

Temperatures on Mars average minus 81 degrees Fahrenheit.

But during wintertime temperatures range from minus 220 degrees Fahrenheit. Lower altitudes in the summer are around +70 degrees, like a comfortable spring day on Earth.

Will they find evidence of life, a destroyed ancient civilization, or beings residing beneath the Martian terrain? The answer is yes, but will NASA allow the Musk's Artemis Mission team to reveal what they find? NASA doesn't want us to know that humans existed on Mars and that aliens reside there.

MARS ANOMALIES

In 1979 or 1980, I had a vision or remote viewing experience, where I stood inside a room at JPL (Jet Propulsion Laboratory) in Pasadena, California, watching engineers and scientists stare at a large monitor hung on the walls. The men were congratulating each other on the image on the monitor of a huge human-looking face structure and other pyramidal structures. Although the images were in black and white, I sensed this was either the Moon or Mars. Oddly, I sensed the building was JPL.

The one interesting image turned out to be the *Face of Mars*, which NASA claimed was a natural geological formation after they altered the image like the strange images on the Moon during the moon missions that a NASA.

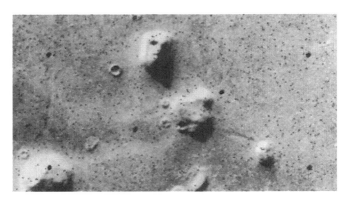

Between 1976 and 1980 the Viking I and Viking II orbiters obtained images and data of the Martian surface that covered the entire planet. One peculiar image captured in 1976 of the Cydonia region, Viking frame 70A13, showed an anomalous mesa with a unique pentagonal shape that caught the attention of two NASA scientists, Vincent DiPietro and Greg Molenaar, titled the *D&M Pyramid*, after their discovery, the formation appeared to express a remarkable set of surface angles. The team remarked that "of all the observations of pyramids on Mars, we find that this one is the most unusual.

Portals and Stargates on Planets

There are portals on Earth, as there are portals throughout the solar system and on planets. Planets have doorways that can be accessed where a planet appears to be devoid of life, once the portal has been entered, life can be seen. Portals are time corridors. Aliens have used these corridors to travel in time and space instantly.

KEYHOLES

Another formation discovered on Mars was equally astounding. Known as the "Exclamation Mark" or "Keyhole" formation was discovered in the Libya Montes region of Mars at approximately 60°N and 92.0°E.

Supportive images are provided by the Mars Odyssey and Mars Reconnaissance Orbiter spacecraft. The images reveal an anomalous structure composed of a triangular and circular component, resembling a keyhole-shaped formation that exhibits a unique set of geometric measurements. The claim of intelligent design was offered but a geologist and geoscientist examined the natural mechanisms that could contribute to the formation of these combined features.

What makes it even stranger is the Keyhole shape is found worldwide among ancient civilizations including ancient Egypt. Ancient Alien theorists have speculated that Mars might have been connected to Earth in the far distant past, and the humans might have lived there before some catastrophic event destroyed them. Did some of the Martians escape to Earth? Keyhole shapes are found in the New World among the Mound Builders, Middle Eastern, Egyptian and Japanese cultures.

The wedge and dome shapes also called the keyhole feature was found to be well-proportioned and symmetrical despite what NASA says was caused by natural depositional and erosional agents. Although there are known geological mechanisms that are capable of creating and destroying angles and planes on the Martian Surface, the keyhole formation and other formations seem to go well beyond the probability of chance.

It is believed that King Solomon has a magical ring that had incredible power. This ring gave Solomon the power to command (demons), jinn, genies, and spirits, or to speak with good spirits as well as animals.

Omm Sety and the Pharoah

Although I wrote about Omm Sety and Pharoah Sety in my last prophecy book, *2021 Looking Into the Future,* I felt the information related to planet Mars and should be included in this book. It's a scary reminder that great civilizations have vanished suddenly on other planets, perhaps from their own stupidity, greed, control, and technology.

This bizarre story is probably too incredible to be believed, but the details in the description are too eerie of Mars to discount. Perhaps the description is Mars where an unknown cataclysmic event killed everyone and all the creatures instantly where they stood.

The love story of Omm Sety and Pharoah Sety was written in the book, *The Search for Omm Sety,* by Jonathan Cott, published in 1987, about the true story of Dorothy Eady, born in England in 1904. At the age of three, Dorothy fell down a flight of stairs and was pronounced dead by Eady's family doctor. Hours later after preparing her body for burial, she awakened as if nothing happened, but Dorothy was changed.

Dorothy began insisting that her parents were not her true parents. After her father had brought home an encyclopedia, the little girl was found reading stories of Egypt and was fascinated with the ancient country. Dorothy began to dream of Egypt with its columns and beautiful gardens and trees. The first time Dorothy was taken to the British Museum in London, she rushed to the Egyptian exhibit and found the mummy of Pharaoh Sety I, refusing to leave. There was something familiar about Sety that she didn't understand.

Through the years, the apparition of Sety I began to appear to her. As an adult, Dorothy eventually married an Egyptian man and moved to Cairo where she worked for the Department of Antiquities in deciphering hieroglyphs. It was during this time that the ghost of Pharaoh Sety began to appear to her on many occasions and he was even witnessed by friends and family. He told her of their love, and they became lovers during his reign when she was a High Priestess. After learning she was pregnant with Sety's child, she committed suicide. After his death, Sety searched for her throughout the cosmos and finally found her reincarnated as Dorothy Eady. Years later, Dorothy Eady became known in Egypt as Omm Sety, *"Mother of Seti."*

Dorothy made this entry in her journal about Sety's visit on August 29, 1974, after he had been absent for 20 days. He told her a story that was both strange and frightening. He told her how maddened he was with sorrow thinking he would never find his beloved.

He said, "I began a search—I reached the skies, and in so doing I found that some, and therefore perhaps all, of the stars were worlds. But they were strange and hateful. Now, Little One (referring to Dorothy), I will tell you the most horrible thing. I found a world in which people had lived. There were great cities with very tall buildings built of large blocks of red stone that had glittering particles in them.

Sety may have been describing the red planet Mars with its deposits of iron rusting on the planet's surface. Rocks and soil on the surface of Mars contain dust composed mostly of iron and small amounts of other elements such as chlorine and sulfur.

"There were fine, wide streets, and some of them had part of the way paved with a shining metal of bright blue. In fact, in the very place where we would have used copper, there was this beautiful blue metal. In the streets lay long metal things with windows and seats inside, but they had neither wings like the metal birds nor wheels. Inside there were people, like us, but much taller, and they were all dead. In the tall houses, in the streets, in the workshops (which had many strange things made of blue metal) were many people, men and women, and children, and all were dead. They were not decayed; their flesh had dried like that of a *sahu* (incorruptible soul*)*. But none of them had any hair on their heads, bodies, or faces. I saw a large, open space like those where the metal birds alight, and there were many of those strange metal things; some of which were full of dead people, some empty, some had people inside, and others about to enter, when they all died.

"One lay at a distance. It was broken, and most of the people in it were broken. They all seem to have died suddenly; each one in his place. Most of them had a look of horror on their faces. It was terrible to behold. Also, I think that they were people of high culture, and they seem to have had many things that the people of the Earth use today. In some houses, I saw pictures made of light. The clothes of the people were strange. They were all alike—men and women, long coverings for the legs and short tunics, and they were made of a strange material that was not woven, but was like papyrus, but seemingly soft and pliable.

"A terrible thing about the place is that there was no air, not a faint breeze stirred. There was no water. Outside the city were vast fields of cultivated plants, all standing dry and motionless, and tall trees, dead and dry, and not a breeze to blow their dry leaves away. There were also some strange-looking animals, all dead, and one still had a mouthful of plants partly in its mouth. I was horrified and sick at heart, and I fled back to *Amenti* (Sety's afterlife world)."

Dorothy had many detailed conversations with Sety on ancient Egypt, Atlantis, and the Pharaoh Akhenaton. The description by Sety during his astral travels to find Dorothy in this distant world was too detailed. Perhaps Sety was describing Mars or a far distant world in our solar system, but whatever caused their demise, natural or unnatural, happened instantly before the beings of this world could escape. Could this explain why many NASA photographs appear to be man-made objects on the surface of Mars, i.e., the Face of Mars, pyramid shapes, miles of glass tubes, that might have been created by technologically advanced beings? The problem appears to be NASA's ability to erase or cover up photographs of objects captured on Mars and then tell us that they are natural formations. So why the big secret and coverup?

Moon Mysteries

Recently, Dr. Ken Johnston, Sr. gave an interesting statement about the Apollo Moon Mission. In 1971, he was a consultant for Brown and Root in the Lunar Receiving Laboratory at the NASA Johnson Center. During this time, he was involved in storing and cataloging Apollo images and also moon rocks. Johnston claims this was when he saw NASA photographs of anomalies and UFOs in the Apollo photos.

Sadly, during this time as mission photos were pouring in with these so-called UFOs and anomalies, Dr. Johnston was witnessing technicians being told to edit them out by painting out the details. These claims were brought to light as Dr. Johnston was donating photographs and other materials to Roswell's International UFO Museum and Research Center.

One of the most shocking claims made by Dr. Johnston was that he was ordered by senior NASA officials to destroy full sets of these photographs. Fortunately, Dr. Johnston was able to hold onto some of these images that showed evidence of unexplained objects and even buildings/structures on the Moon. Obviously, NASA denies any doctoring to remove any evidence of aliens or UFOs. NASA still claims that they have not found any evidence of life outside of our planet, which is a lie.

The Hopi people have a legend about the Ant People who saved them from starving. Some believe the Ant People left Earth for the Moon, during a time it was a natural satellite. Through the thousands of years, the Moon was destroyed by invading aliens, and so the Ant People had to build a new moon, for the continuity of their evolutionary process.

The construction of the new artificial Moon took thousands of years to build. That is why there are sharp edges, geometric structures, and signs of engineering on the Moon's surface.

It sounds crazy but not when you consider that between 1972 and 1977, NASA installed seismometers on the Moon to record moonquakes. Deep moonquakes happen extremely often, typically on a cycle of roughly 27 days, and occur nearly 700 km below the surface of the moon. Most believe that the quakes are caused by the tidal pull of Earth on the moon. When the frozen crust suddenly expands, it can cause a moonquake. But what if the quakes are not natural but from a base beneath the Moon's surface?

The Moon was described as "ringing like a bell" during some of those quakes, specifically the shallow ones. When Apollo 12 deliberately crashed the Ascent Stage of its Lunar Module onto the Moon's surface, NASA claimed that the Moon rang like a bell for one-hour, leading conspiracy theorists to suggest that the Moon was hollow and perhaps an artificial satellite. Vast chambers beneath the Moon could also explain the hollow ringing. (Refer to Betsey's *2021 Looking Into the Future* on Amazon to learn more about the Ant People).

CHAPTER 7

PLANET X

Mike Brown and Konstantin Batygin, of the California Institute of Technology (Caltech) in Pasadena, California, were prepared for the inevitable skepticism with detailed analyses of its orbit and months of computer simulations. "If you say, 'We have evidence for Planet X,' almost any astronomer will say, 'This again? These guys are clearly crazy.' I would, too," Brown said. "Why is this different? This difference is because this time we're right."

Brown and Batygin said that astronomers should be able to find more objects in telltale orbits, shaped by the pull of the hidden giant. But Brown knows that no one will believe in the discovery until Planet X itself appears within a telescope viewfinder. "Until there's a direct detection, it's a hypothesis— even a potentially very good hypothesis," he said.

It's harder to explain why Planet X didn't either loop back around to where it started or leave the solar system entirely, but we know that most solar systems appear to have binary stars/suns, and Planet X might have been this solar system's second sun, that cooled and became a "Brown Dwarf" or failed star between 3 million and 10 million years ago. Now it's caught in an orbit through our solar system every 6,000 to 15,000 years.

Shortly after Brown and Batygin revealed the 9th planet, possibly Planet X, few articles were released on the subject.

Don't expect our leaders to admit to Planet X's journey through our solar systems and how it is responsible for our extreme weather, increased seismic and volcanic activity.

Interesting news recently shows that between South America and southern Africa, there is an enigmatic magnetic region called the South Atlantic Anomaly, where the magnetic field is a lot stranger than expected. Scientists believe that weak and unstable fields are thought to precede magnetic reversals and they might happen at any time. A study, published on June 12, 2020, by the National Academy of Sciences, uncovered how long the field in the South Atlantic has been acting up. This might be a harbinger of a physical shift of the poles.

What scientists are sure of is that a weak magnetic field makes Earth more prone to magnetic storms that can knock out the electronic infrastructure, including the power grids.

The magnetic field of the South Atlantic Anomaly is already so weak that it has affected satellites and their technology when they fly past it. The strange region is related to the magnetic field that points in a different directions.

Geologists at Rice University have uncovered evidence that suggests Earth's spin axis was in a different spot millions of years ago, a phenomenon called "true polar wander." The change happened around 12 million years ago and shifted Greenland further up into the Arctic Circle, which may have contributed to the onset of the last major Ice Age, 3.2 million years ago.

This axle has always stayed the same relative to the sun, giving our planet its characteristic axial tilt. But the North and South poles haven't always been the same. It shows at various times in our planet's history that the true poles have been in different places. New evidence of these shifts comes from an analysis of millions of years of data left behind in Earth's geological record—in the path of hotspots in Hawaii and sediments and magnetic fields taken from the seafloor.

Scientists found that between 48 million and about 12 million years ago, the Earth's spin axis, and therefore the geographic north and south poles, were in a different place than they are today. Long ago, the North Pole would have been closer to Greenland than it is now, and the South Pole would have shifted similarly to the west. Somewhere around 12 million years ago, the poles moved to where they are now.

Although geologists speculate that a massive asteroid hit the earth 65 million years ago and caused the extinction of the dinosaur, it might have caused an imbalance in the Earth's poles and caused them to change places.

Is there any evidence that the Sun once rose in the west and set in the east, the reverse of today? If the sun did rise in the west, this would certainly add more evidence of our planet flipping or reverse of the Earth's rotation and hemispheres. If such a mega event occurred, our ancestors would have put down some form of ancient written or oral legend of this event.

Immanuel Velikovsky in his *World in Collision* book investigated ancient records that show evidence for a reversing of the sun rising and setting in ancient Egyptian records. Herodotus, the ancient Greek historian, wrote that four times during this period the sun rose contrary to his, twice it rose where it now set, and twice it set where it now rises.

Pomponius Mela, a Latin author of the first century wrote: "The Egyptians pride themselves on being the most ancient people in the world. In their authentic annals, one may read that since they have been in existence, the course of the stars has changed direction four times and that the sun has set twice in that part of the sky where it rises today."

The magical Papyrus Harris is the longest known papyrus from Egypt, with some 1,500 lines of text. It was found in a tomb near Medinet Habu, across the Nile River from Luxor, Egypt in 1855, and was sent to the British Museum in 1872. The ancient text speaks of a cosmic upheaval of fire and water when "the south becomes north, and the Earth turns over." In the Papyrus Ipuwer, it also tells of a great catastrophic event, and states that "the land turns around [over] as does a potter's wheel" and the "Earth turned upside down."

In the Egyptian tomb of Senmut, the architect of Queen Hatshepsut, a panel on the ceiling shows the celestial sphere with the signs of the zodiac and other constellations in "a reversed orientation" of the southern sky.

Caius Julius Solinus, a Latin author of the third century, wrote of the people living on the southern borders of Egypt, "The inhabitants of this country say that they have it from their ancestors the sun now sets where it formerly rose."

In the Syrian city of Ugarit (Ras Shamra) a poem was discovered dedicated to the planet-goddess Anat, who massacred the population of the Levant and who exchanged the two dawns and the position of the Stars.

The ancient Maya of Mexico wrote in hieroglyphics describing four movements of the sun, *'nahui ollin tonatiugh.'* These four motions refer to four prehistoric suns or world ages, with shifting cardinal points.

It's beyond coincidence that both the Egyptians and the ancient people of Mexico also referred to four events.

The Eskimos of Greenland related their legends to missionaries that in ancient times the Earth turned over and the people who lived then became antipodes. (The meaning of antipode is related to geography and any spot point on Earth's surface diametrically opposite to it).

Lastly, the Koran speaks of the Lord of two easts and two wests.

This shows that the people who run our world don't want us to know what is taking place on our planet and outside our planet.

On September 10, 1984, a news report from US News World questioned if Planet X was really out there. The report read that in 1983, the infrared astronomical satellite (IRAS), circling the polar orbit 560 miles from the Earth, detected heat from an object about 50 billion miles away that is now the subject of intense speculation. "All I can say is that we don't know what it is yet," said Gerry Neugebauer, director of the Palomar Observatory for the California Institute of Technology.

Then in 1992, NASA issued a press release, "Unexplained deviations in the orbits of Uranus and Neptune point to a large outer solar system body of 4 to 8 Earth masses on a highly tilted orbit, beyond 7billion miles from the Sun." A follow-up released stated, "Astronomers are so sure of the 10th planet, they think there is nothing left but to name it," stated Ray T. Reynolds, a researcher at NASA in a press release 1992.

Oddly, these stories were quickly retracted without any explanation.

In December of 2015, I posted my predictions on my website and wrote, *"Watch for NASA to announce more weird news on the planets and astonishing finds in our solar system and beyond. They are going to make some outrageous claims and maybe even an alien disclosure about ancient structures in outer space—Mars and the Moon."*

Then the most incredible news happened on January 20, 2016—two Caltech scientists, Brown and Batygin, gave a press conference and announced they had discovered the ninth planet in our solar system, 10 times the size of Earth. They believed it was Planet X. They calculated the massive body orbits the sun every 15,000 years.

Mike Brown and Konstantin Batygin, of the California Institute of Technology (Caltech) in Pasadena, California, were prepared for the inevitable skepticism with detailed analyses of its orbit and months of computer simulations. "If you say, 'We have evidence for Planet X,' almost any astronomer will say, 'This again? These guys are clearly crazy.' I would, too," Brown said. "Why is this different? This different because this time we're right."

If Planet X is out there, Brown and Batygin said that astronomers should find more objects in telltale orbits, shaped by the pull of the hidden giant. But Brown knows that no one will believe in the discovery until Planet X itself appears within a telescope viewfinder. "Until there's a direct detection, it's a hypothesis—even a potentially very good hypothesis," he said.

It's harder to explain why Planet X didn't either loop back around to where it started or leave the solar system entirely, but we know that most solar systems appear to have binary stars/suns, and Planet X might have been this solar system's second sun, that cooled and became a "Brown Dwarf" or failed star between 3 million and 10 million years ago. Now it's caught in an orbit through our solar system every 6,000 to 15,000 years.

Shortly after Brown and Batygin revealed the 9th planet, possibly Planet X, few articles were released on the subject.

Don't expect our leaders to admit to Planet X's journey through our solar systems and that it might be responsible for our extreme weather, increased seismic and volcanic activity. Already people are photographing a second huge object near the sun at dusk (check out YouTube videos).

Do I believe Planet X is out there and traveling through our Solar System? Absolutely! In the past few years, NASA has made comments on strange anomalies on the planet in our solar system without any explanation. If anything can cause our planet to shift its pole, it would be the strong magnetic pull from this supergiant.

Nancy Lieder of ZetaTalk claims she was told by Zeta extraterrestrials that Planet X will cause our planet to shift again as it has in the past. She further stated Earth would slow its rotation and stop for a few hours. One half of the Earth's hemisphere will be in total darkness (night) and the other half in sunlight. Within hours, the shift will take place and there will be hurricane-force winds, powerful earthquakes will shake the Earth for days, volcanoes will erupt and dormant volcanoes dormant will awaken. Coastal areas globally will be inundated by oceans. The safety areas in the United States will be the Southwest, areas of the Midwest, and places away from the West and East coasts. Look for areas with old geology.

Nancy has gotten geological and weather predictions right, but the Zetas were wrong about the shift happening in the 1990s.

Nancy Lieder recently posted on her website that the Council of Worlds plans to allow a severe wobble on Earth to force the establishment to admit the reality of Nibiru. Was the mega eruption of the Tonga volcano a warning by the Council? In that such a temporary Severe Wobble would have to merge in with the daily Earth Wobble, it is a tricky affair for the benign aliens arranging to fulfill the Council's edict. Photos from April 2021 to the present show that Nibiru's North Pole has been tilted to point UP, temporarily, where formerly was pointing at the Earth.

What this change does is ease the Daily Earth Wobble temporarily, while giving benign aliens the tools they need to affect a Severe Wobble. By suddenly allowing the magnetic flow surrounding Nibiru to change, allowing Nibiru's North Pole to drop and point again at the Earth, a mega wobble would be affected. This would be noticed by everyone on Earth, and the establishment would be scrambling to explain it. This temporarily Severe Wobble would be accompanied by dramatic visibility of Nibiru so that the usual excuses from NASA that the wobble was somehow from the Sun would not suffice.

Even the late prophet Edgar Cayce (1877-1945) who gave thousands of readings in a trance-like state foretold of an Earth shift in the year 2000. Thankfully, his prediction has yet to come true.

If my recurring dreams of great earth changes at the age of seven prove to be correct, it would happen later in my adult lifetime—that could be in the next few years. I have been shown there will be signs and warnings before the Earth shifts.

Mount Graham in Arizona is one of the most sacred and holiest places for the Apache and it's believed to be a stargate or portal for deities and other-worldly entities to enter our world.

The Vatican Observatory Research Group or-VORG) operates the 1.8m Alice P. Lennon Telescope with its Thomas J. Bannan Astrophysics Facility, known together as the Vatican Advanced Technology Telescope or VATT, at the Mount Graham International Observatory (MGIO) in southeastern Arizona where sky conditions are among the best in the world and certainly the Continental United States. Mt. Graham is near Tucson, Arizona, in the Apache San Carlos reservation. At 3200 meters it is one of the highest peaks in Arizona. Above all, though, it is the single most sacred site of the Apache Nation.

Mount Graham or *Dzil Nchaa Si An*, known by the local natives as 'Big Seated Mountain' because of its distinctive profile, is an important religious reference point for the Apache: their ancestors are buried there; their medicine-men go there to collect therapeutic herbal plants, and the Apache shamans perform their sacred rites there.

The Apache and extraterrestrials seem to be linked in other ways. The Apache Indians have a great dislike for owls and that goes back to their legends. The owl, the snake, and the coyote are considered evil to them. Could there be a stargate on Mount Graham for extraterrestrials?

Alien abductees worldwide have recalled seeing an owl during their abduction. Owls, amongst other animals, often appear as a disguise to replace the images of the actual alien abductions and medical examinations that took place. And it is suspected that these screen memories were implanted within the abductees by the aliens to prevent mental trauma from the abduction.

The Apache tribal members website states they tried to sue the University of Arizona, the Vatican, and the Jesuit Order to cease the building and desecration of their mountain but lost their fight (what a surprise!).

Author and Researcher of ancient mythology and paranormal phenomena Tom Horn discussed his visit to the Arizona observatory on the *Coast to Coast* talk radio show on March 25, 2013. He stated that Jesuit Brother Guy Consolmagno, astronomer to the Vatican, said the Vatican had nothing to do with the telescope's naming. German astronomers were responsible for the name L.U.C.I.F.E.R, which is an acronym for "Large Binocular Telescope Near-infrared Utility with Camera and Integral Field Unit for Extragalactic Research."

Many critics claim the Lucifer telescope shows the Vatican's loyalty to their true master—Lucifer or Satan, by using God and Jesus as shills to hide their deception.

What was the Vatican searching for? Many conspiracy theorists speculate its "wormwood" which appears several times in the Old Testament from the Hebrew term לענה (la'anah). The only time the word is used is in the New Testament and the book of Revelation: *The third angel blew his trumpet, and a great star fell from heaven, blazing like a torch, and it fell on a third of the rivers and on the springs of water. The name of the star is Wormwood. A third of the waters became wormwood, and many died from the water because it was made bitter.* (Revelation 8:10–11).

On New Year's eve 1949, Padre Pio had a powerful vision given to him by Jesus Christ concerning the three days of darkness.

"My Son, my love for man is very great, especially for those who give themselves to me...The time is near at hand in which I shall visit my unfaithful people because they have not heeded the time of my grace. My judgment shall come upon them suddenly and when least expected—no one shall escape My hands. But I shall protect the just. Watch the sun and moon and the stars, when they appear unduly disturbed and restless, know that the day is not far away.

"Stay united in prayer and watch until the Angel of Destruction has passed your doors. Pray that these days will be shortened. My children have confidence, I am in the midst of you. My Kingdom shall be glorified, and My Name shall be blessed from the rising of the sun unto the setting. My Kingdom shall have no end.

"Pray! Men are running toward the abyss of Hell in great rejoicing and merry making, as though to a masquerade ball or the wedding feast of the devil himself. Assist Me in the salvation of souls. The measure of sin is filled! The day of revenge, with its terrifying happenings is near! Nearer than you can imagine! And the world is sleeping in false security! The Divine Judgment shall strike them like a thunderbolt! These godless and wicked people shall be destroyed without mercy, as were the inhabitants of Sodom and Gomorrah of old. Yes, I tell you their wickedness was not as great as that of our human race of today!

"This catastrophe shall come upon the earth like a flash of lightning! at which moment the light of the morning sun shall be replaced by black darkness! No one shall leave the house or look out of a window from that moment on. I shall come amidst thunder and lightning. The wicked shall behold My Divine Heart. There shall be great confusion because of this utter darkness in which the entire earth shall be enveloped. And many, many shall die from fear and despair. Those who shall fight for My cause shall receive grace from My Divine Heart; and the cry: 'WHO IS LIKE UNTO GOD!" shall serve as a means of protection to many. However, many shall burn in the open fields like withered grass! The godless shall be annihilated, so that afterward the just shall be able to start afresh.

"ON THAT DAY, AS SOON AS COMPLETE DARKNESS has set in, no one shall leave the house or look from out of the window. The darkness shall last a day and a night, followed by another day and a night, and another day--but on the night following, the stars will shine again, and on the next morning the sun shall rise again, and it will be Springtime!

"In the days of darkness, my elect shall not sleep, as did the disciples in the garden of olives. They shall pray incessantly, and they shall not be disappointed in Me. I shall gather My elect. Hell will believe itself to be in possession of the entire earth, but I shall reclaim it.

"Those who disregard this advice will be killed instantly. The wind will carry with it poisonous gases which will be diffused over the entire earth. Those who suffer and die innocently will be martyrs and they will be with Me in My Kingdom. Satan will triumph! But in three nights, the earthquake and fire will cease. On the following day, the sun *will shine again, angels will descend from Heaven and will spread the spirit of peace over the earth. A feeling of immeasurable gratitude will take possession of those who survive this most terrible ordeal, the impending punishment, with which God will visit the earth since creation.*

Was Padre Pio's prophecy about Planet X's passage through our solar system accompanied by a super solar event?

In Ray Stanford's book, *Fatima Prophecy*, copyright 1987, he discussed Padre Pio's prophecy and his own channeled information in 1972 about a solar event. He describes cosmic energy and particle which, in the not-distant future, will collide with the sun and planets and energize the ionosphere of planets and the earth's atmosphere. According to Stanford, the cosmic rays encountering the sun and planetary body of the Earth would cause a chemical reaction in the ionosphere. The reaction of the sun itself would cause a great enhancement and increase of solar winds, atomic hydrogen moving through space, and of other isotopic substances carried by magnetic fields to the Earth and other planets, encountering and affecting even the atmosphere.

Stanford compared the Fatima "Dancing Sun" event on October 13, 1917, to the Bible's three days of darkness and Padre Pio's vision of Jesus Christ. Padre Pio warned that we must close our doors and windows and never open them or go out, or we will die. The radioactivity itself from the cosmic-solar event would kill the human body. He goes on to say, "The spinning symbolizes the drunkenness and chaos by which men shall respond to the darkness of the sun and the energies that it emits. The strange colors there at Fatima symbolize the strange energies and rays which the sun shall affect upon the Earth, the colors and fires which shall come even in the skies and from the clouds.

"What is more, those that survive [the cosmic event] shall have been changed, even though they remain within their houses, where they must pray and meditate all during this event if they are to find the emotional strength not to go mad or to die of a signal through the autonomic system that would kill the body.

"Even the genetic pattern in many of these will be changed. A new race of man shall have begun. *The evolution of man shall have been enhanced.* The offspring shall change in their appearance. Strange shall be their eyes, and a new tendency for a different coloration of the eye, varying from the normal eye colorations as known [at the present time]. There shall be a reshaping, to some extent, of the basic proportions of the body and of the cranium [alien-like?].

"This is the new root race of man, preparing for the reappearance of repentant souls, purged by those things which they have seen. Thereby, entities may come and incarnate again (when their bodies are made ready), and worship the Lord in body, thus in Spirit, thus in truth."

Prophecy 2022

There is a longing among all people and creatures to have a sense of purpose and worth. To satisfy that common longing in all of us we must respect each other. —Chief Dan George

CHAPTER 8

WISDOM OF THE INDIGENOUS

Chief Dan George was a leader of the Tsleil-Waututh Nation as well as a beloved actor, musician, poet, and author. He was born in North Vancouver in 1899 and died in 1981. He wrote the following in 1972.

"In the course of my lifetime, I have lived in two distinct cultures. I was born into a culture that lived in communal houses. My grandfather's house was eighty feet long. It was called a smoke house, and it stood down by the beach along the inlet. All my grandfather's sons and their families lived in this dwelling. Their sleeping apartments were separated by blankets made of bull rush weeds, but one open fire in the middle served the cooking needs of all.

"In houses like these, throughout the tribe, people learned to live with one another; learned to respect the rights of one another. And children shared the thoughts of the adult world and found themselves surrounded by aunts, uncles, and cousins who loved them and did not threaten them. My father was born in such a house and learned from infancy how to love people and be at home with them.

"And beyond this acceptance of one another, there was a deep respect for everything in Nature that surrounded them. My father loved the Earth and all its creatures. The Earth was his second mother. The Earth and everything it contained was a gift from See-see-am... and the way to thank this Great Spirit was to use his gifts with respect.

"I remember, as a little boy, fishing with him up Indian River and I can still see him as the sun rose above the mountain top in the early morning...I can see him standing by the water's edge with his arms raised above his head while he softly moaned, 'Thank you, thank you.' It left a deep impression on my young mind.

"And I shall never forget his disappointment when once he caught me gaffing for fish "just for the fun of it." "My son," he said, "The Great Spirit gave you those fish to be your brothers, to feed you when you are hungry. You must respect them. You must not kill them just for the fun of it."

"This then was the culture I was born into and for some years the only one I really knew or tasted. This is why I find it hard to accept many of the things I see around me. I see people living in smoke houses hundreds of times bigger than the one I knew. But the people in one apartment do not even know the people in the next and care less about them.

"It is also difficult for me to understand the deep hate that exists among people. It is hard to understand a culture that justifies the killing of millions in past wars, and at this very moment preparing bombs to kill even greater numbers. It is hard for me to understand a culture that spends more on wars and weapons to kill than it does on education and welfare to help and develop. It is hard for me to understand a culture that not only hates and fights his brothers but even attacks Nature and abuses her. I see my white brothers going about blotting out Nature from his cities. I see him strip the hills bare, leaving ugly wounds on the face of mountains. I see him tearing things from the bosom of Mother Earth as though she were a monster, who refused to share her treasures with him. I see him throw poison in the waters, indifferent to the life he kills there; as he chokes the air with deadly fumes.

"My white brother does many things well for he is more clever than my people but I wonder if he has ever really learned to love at all. Perhaps he only loves the things that are his own but never learned to love the things that are outside and beyond him. And this is, of course, not love at all, for man must love all creation or he will love none of it. Man must love fully or he will become the lowest of the animals. It is the power to love that makes him the greatest of them all... for he alone of all animals is capable of [a deeper] love.

"My friends, how desperately do we need to be loved and to love. When Christ said man does not live by bread alone, he spoke of a hunger. This hunger was not the hunger of the body. He spoke of a hunger that begins in the very depths of man... a hunger for love. Love is something you and I must have. We must have it because our spirit feeds upon it. We must have it because without it we become weak and faint. Without love, our self-esteem weakens. Without it, our courage fails. Without love, we can no longer look out confidently at the world. Instead, we turn inwardly and begin to feed upon our own personalities, and little by little we destroy ourselves.

"You and I need the strength and joy that comes from knowing that we are loved. With it we are creative. With it, we march tirelessly. With it, and with it alone, we are able to sacrifice for others. There have been times when we all wanted so desperately to feel a reassuring hand upon us... there have been lonely times when we so wanted a strong arm around us... I cannot tell you how deeply I miss my wife's presence when I return from a trip. Her love was my greatest joy, my strength, my greatest blessing.

"I am afraid my culture has little to offer yours. But my culture did prize friendship and companionship. It did not look on privacy as a thing to be clung to, for privacy builds walls and walls promote distrust. My culture lived in big family communities, and from infancy, people learned to live with others.

"My culture did not prize the hoarding of private possessions, in fact, to hoard was a shameful thing to do among my people. The Indian looked on all things in Nature as belonging to him and he expected to share them with others and to take only what he needed.

Everyone likes to give as well as receive. No one wishes only to receive all the time. We have taken something from your culture... I wish you had taken something from our culture, for there were some beautiful and good things in it.

"Soon it will be too late to know my culture, for integration is upon us and soon we will have no values but yours. Already many of our young people have forgotten the old ways. And many have been shamed of their Indian ways by scorn and ridicule. My culture is like a wounded deer that has crawled away into the forest to bleed and die alone.

"The only thing that can truly help us is genuine love. You must truly love, be patient with us and share with us. And we must love you—with a genuine love that forgives and forgets... a love that forgives the terrible sufferings your culture brought ours when it swept over us like a wave crashing along a beach... with a love that forgets and lifts up its head and sees in your eyes an answering love of trust and acceptance..."

For thousands of years Australian Aboriginals have lived in harmony with Mother Earth, but there was a time long before they arrived on Earth, they came from a far distant place in the stars, according to their ancient legends. In Steven McFadden's book, *Ancient Voices, Current Affairs: The Legend of The Rainbow Warriors,* he cited the late Australian Aboriginal leader, visionary, activist, and filmmaker, Alinta aka Lorraine Mafi Williams, and her wise words to the world. Their legend speaks of the importance of maintaining the Earth's grid and vibrational rate.

Time to tell everyone

We, the Australian Aboriginals, have been on our traditional land, the Land of the Everlasting Spirit, for tens of thousands of years. Our culture is rivaled by no other, though we have been in seclusion for the last two hundred years. We are re-emerging from that seclusion now to show ourselves as no one has ever seen us.

Our creation stories take us back into Dreamtime, beginning when the Earth was one land mass. At that time the four races—red, yellow, black, and white, lived side by side. There, they lived as one people, creating a world of harmony, balance and mystery.

As Aboriginals we have kept our culture intact for

thousands of years into the present time. Now we are ready to share our wondrous culture with the other people of the world. That is my work through my teaching and my films.

It took the white people only fifty years to destroy a million years of our culture, but the core of it still remains strong. We haven't forgotten. Our elders are telling us to go out and tell everyone, so that no one can say they didn't hear.

Land of the everlasting spirit

Whenever our elders or shaman people—all our elders are shaman people—talk about our history and our beginning, our creation, they always talk about the time when the Earth was one land mass. They speak of the time before the cataclysm came that split the Earth up into continents.

This is our story, our mythology. Our land, Australia is called Arunta, the Land of the Everlasting Spirit. Our old people tell us that we originally came from a planet that had seen its time and just blew up.

See, our people were like refugees, and they went and lived in the stars in the Milky Way. Then seven spirit brothers and seven spirit sisters came to Earth. They came when the Earth was one big land mass.

They came to erect an energy grid. Because you see, the planet Earth is among the smallest of planets. And it is really not in the galactic system where all the other planets exist. We believe Earth is just a little bit outside the plane of the Milky Way galaxy in space. Because the Earth is so small, when the planets line up in a certain way, the pull of the galactic energy is so strong that it could just suck planet Earth into the spiral plane of the galactic system and toss it all around.

So, my people were given the knowledge to create this energy grid because the planet that they were previously on did not have such a protective structure, and it was destroyed. They realized that their new home, Earth, needed to have such an energy grid in a strong, healthy condition to withstand periodic energy pulsations from the galaxy.

Otherwise, it would quickly be drawn into the plane of the galaxy and experience devastating turbulence.

But my ancestors had learned this lesson, and so they came to Earth to erect an energy grid, or an Earth truss, to help the Earth when it undergoes its changes.

The Sacred Rainbow Serpent

In our old way, we call the energy grid Boamie, the Sacred Rainbow Serpent, whose colors reflect the beauty of the Earth and sky, the Rainbows. The multicolored coils of the Rainbow Serpent are reflected in the precious stones that are concealed in the Earth's crust. It is called the Rainbow Serpent because it has all the colors of the rainbow, gold, and silver, of course, and the diamonds, the rubies, the emeralds, and the uranium. You see, it is the foundation, the Earth's crust. They are the particular substances that keep the energy grid strong and the Earth solid when the planets line up every so often and threaten to draw the Earth into the galactic energy swirl.

Since my people erected the energy grid, the Earth just sort of sails through the periodic planetary lineups without any difficulties. So that's my people's responsibility. Both men and women are very knowledgeable in how the energy grid works for the whole system. We know what each mineral on the Earth is supposed to do, and what men's and women's responsibilities are to keep the grid strong and healthy.

Earth's balance is in jeopardy

We are very concerned about the energy grids of the Earth. They are there to help the Earth maintain its balance. Crystals and other minerals feed energy to the energy grid. They have been used for millions of years that way. For the health of the Earth, the crystals must be free to let the energy flow to the grid.

But now minerals, metals, and jewels have been removed from the Earth to such an extent that the balance is in jeopardy. Uranium, in particular, is important for this task. When it is all gone, the Earth will be right out of balance.

The mining has an influence on the human race, too, and the human body. The human being is a link between the Heavens and the Earth. By keeping our bodies in balance and in harmony, we can keep the Earth healthy, and that in turn supports our health. You see, it's a cycle. I used crystals in healing, but I do not believe they should be taken from the Earth to be used as ornaments. It's more valuable to leave them in the Earth. The same applies to uranium.

At a crucial juncture

We have been told that within everyone million years, there is a seven-thousand-year-long Earth shift. Then we begin to go into a new world like we are doing now. By our reckoning, we are actually at the end of a seven-thousand-year shift now and we are beginning to enter a new million-year-long epoch.

Our people and our teachings are very similar to the teachings of the North American Indians. But we have different interpretations, and we know our responsibility—taking care of the Earth through the energy grids. We perform our task by giving thanks to the Earth through songs, dances, and ceremonies.

Right now, there are two things. The Earth is undergoing its earthly changes, which is normal for this time in our development. But because there's been so much destruction to the energy grid, especially the gold, which is nearly exhausted already—and now they are after the uranium—there is a great danger to the stability of the Earth.

Gold has driven men mad for thousands of years, leading them to lie, steal, cheat, murder, and make war...all this wickedness to get the gold. Humanity has become greedy and as a result, wicked. That has led to fighting, war, and disease. People have forgotten their responsibility to the Earth, for want of the gold. And now it's the uranium.

As well as the Earth, humanity has to go through its changes. We've all got to rejuvenate and create a new world on the same physical substance. And we are going through it. There's no safe place on Earth. We've just got to ride it out, but if we are in balance within ourselves and in balance with the Earth, then we are healthy.

At the end of each change—every time we come into a new world—the Great Creator says: 'OK humanity, you must start your change now, too, and go into the new world—but you must do it in accordance with the Earth, as well as yourself, with heart.

Like the Australian Aboriginals and their legend, they came from the stars, the Maya of Mesoamerica speak of a time when they came from the stars.

We are all from the stars. I've heard too many people say they don't feel Earth is their true home, and it's not.

Nonviolence is a powerful and just weapon, which cuts without wounding and ennobles the man who wields it. It is a sword that heals. – Martin Luther King

CHAPTER 9

ALL LIVES MATTER

I grew up in a different era of ideals than the youth of today. I've always believed that all life matters, all races matter unlike those who espouse violence in our world. The truth is that a Creator that we acknowledge as God, Great Spirit, Supreme Beings, Brahman, Jehovah, Allah, and many other names, created us in his/her image and that means we are all equal. We are part of the mystery of God and we all matter! No one is better than another human because of their skin color, ethnicity, their religious beliefs, their financial worth, their social stature, education, or sexual preference. Everything matters in our physical world—the trees, the plants, the insects, the ocean creature, the four-legged creatures, the birds, and humans.

BLM (Black Lives Matter) supporters and some black Congressional Democrats took the arrogant stance that only they mattered, and no one else—not Whites, Asians, Native Americans, East Indians, Aboriginals, and all other nationalities—just them.

I find that the millennials born between 1981 and 1996 are the angry ones who feel they are entitled to everything and anything. Mostly young people rioted in 2,000 major U.S. cities in 2020 after George Floyd, a known criminal, was killed after a police officer placed his knee on his neck. Floyd was high on the illegal drugs fentanyl and methamphetamine at the time, which also contributed to his death.

Floyd became an instant martyr to the youth of America and worldwide. But how can a criminal and drug abuser become a hero? But he did.

BLM and Antifa rioters took to the streets and looted, set fire to businesses and cars, causing an estimated $500 million in property damages, besides what they stole. According to Forbes Magazine, 19 people were killed during 14 days of protests and riots. Some were arrested, but most were bailed out and have never been convicted. House Speaker Nancy Pelosi and Vice president Kamala Harris appeared on television in support of the rioters, yet they have condoned January 6 as an insurrection compared to World War II Pearl Harbor and the Civil War.

What kind of government encourages people to riot?

Something different happened on January 6, 2021, in Washington, D.C. that is now called a terrorist act or "insurrection," yet looting, setting fire to businesses burning them to the ground, and killing innocent people in major cities was never considered a terrorist act or insurrection. That's because the majority of U.S. citizens were brainwashed into believing that January 6, 2021, was worse than what BLM did in the summer of 2020 in major cities.

Five people died on January 6, 2021—four died from heart attacks or natural causes and Ashli Babbitt, a military veteran of 14 years, was the only person shot in the back of the neck by a black Capitol Policeman as she tried to climb through a broken window leading to the Capitol Chamber. She was unarmed. Yet, January 6 was dubbed an "Insurrection" or coup, and compared to the Pearl Harbor bombings by Japan during World War II where over 2,400 military and civilians died and the Civil War from 1861 to 1865 that killed an estimated 750,000 soldiers. January 6, 2021, in Washington, D.C. was not an insurrection by any means, but the major media pushed their lies on the public that it was.

They wanted to anger people to create more violence to

further their dark agenda and bring about martial law.

Certain disguised MAGA men were planted among the Trump protestors to push them toward the Capitol building. There were police removing barriers and waving Trump protestors through to the Capitol.

Ray Epps, whoever he is, instructed protesters to enter the U.S. Capitol Building on January 5, and later shepherded crowds toward the Capitol on January 6. Turned out he was probably a Federal Protected provocateur. But who hired him and why hasn't he been prosecuted like masses of Trump supporters who did nothing that day, but attend the rally for Trump?

Ray Epps has never been questioned in Congress about his role on January 6.

Another red-faced man in MAGA clothes encouraged Trump supporters to move on the Capitol as they shouted out "Fed, Fed", and another unidentified man posing as a Trump supporter passed out mace, hammers, and clubs to Trump supporters and told them to push to the Capitol. Congress in their committee investigations of January 6 have refused to release all the film footage of what took place that day.

Ask yourself what are they hiding from the American public?

African Americans have been mistreated through the years by police and they had a right to protest even if George Floyd's death was due to both a policeman kneeling on his neck and the drugs in his body. But other races have been discriminated against throughout the history of America—Native Americans, the Irish, Germans, the English, Jewish people, Polish people, Asians, East Indians, and on and on.

Suddenly after January 6, people were banned from social media sites, books were banned, statues representing our history were torn down, and everything turned black. Almost all commercials on television represent the black race. It's as if all other races were removed from the Earth. Where is equality for all? Instead, it's become equity, not equality for all nationalities.

The major media, owned by major corporations, control what news reporters write and speak. They no longer have a voice in the news, but parroted what others say or what they are told.

Kyle Rittenhouse was defamed by the major media, and his corrupt attorneys claimed he was part of a militia while taking millions of dollars donated to him during his trial.

I don't mean to make this into a political book, but I wanted to point out how most of the public has been fooled by unethical Leftist politicians, news journalists, and reporters. The truth is you can't believe what our politicians, news people, and government tell you. We should always question what we are told, and that includes COVID-19 and the vaccines. There is a definite dark agenda afoot.

These events affect our future and the generations that will hopefully carry-on America's democracy.

The Truth about Kyle Rittenhouse
I watched Fox's Tucker Carlson's full interview with Kyle Rittenhouse on Monday, November 22, 2021, and I could see what an upstanding young man Kyle is at age 18. He's polite, sincere, articulate, and smart beyond his age. Kyle Rittenhouse was unjustly accused of being part of a militia by his first two corrupt attorneys who took close to million dollars from him and didn't bother to have him released from jail on bail. It was all about the attorney's cause. The Major News mob grabbed that info and ran with it. They wanted to make this a racist event, but Kyle didn't go to Kenosha to attack anyone. He went there to protect car lots being burned by rioters. He was cleaning graffiti off of the walls of stores during the riot while police stood by and did nothing! Kyle turned himself into the police. Eventually, he was jailed for 87 days where he had no access to running water. He couldn't bathe for a month!

Kyle was attacked by several people during the riot in 2020- -hit in the head by a skateboard, kicked and threatened by certain people, some pointing guns at him. He killed two criminal white men (Rosenbaum was a convicted felon), not black men as the major media echoed everywhere. There was so much disinformation about Kyle it's a miracle that he received a fair trial.

As Kyle said it wasn't about racism, it was about self-defense, and having the right to defend yourself in this country when attacked.

Kyle's situation is the perfect example of home an incident can be created, then exploited in the media, to create bitter political divisions and distract the public from the real issues— inflation, the border crisis, the COVID-19 vaccine misinformation, and the unrest in Afghanistan, China, North Korea, and Russia. If you switched channels to MSNBC, CNN,

ABC, NBC, CBS news you heard them all say the same thing—Kyle had an AK-47, he crossed borders, he came from a militia background, and he killed three African Americans. Kyle had an AK-15, he shot two white felons and injured another white man after he was attacked by all three.

We are inundated daily with extremist left-right propaganda from Congress, the Senate, Biden, VP Kama Harris, and major news organizations. They want you constantly fearful and divided. This is all about neurolinguistic programming to effectively change people's behaviors without their conscious knowledge. It's mind-control.

Kyle's Astrology

As an astrologer, I looked up Kyle's birthday on January 3, 2003, and sensed that what happened in Kenosha during the trial was divine guidance. Kyle has much to do in life—he has a calm Zen demeanor and here's why: His special star Pelagus, also known as Nunki, bestows a love of truthfulness, a strong character, and a direct and assertive manner. His star imparts sound common sense and determination to achieve success (he is attending college and hope to be a nurse or get into law). I foresee him getting into law. His star urges him toward higher learning, especially in philosophy, history, and spirituality. He imparts an outspoken personality and strong convictions. It shows he will rise in an influential public position later in life and he will make a positive name for himself where he could become involved in complex situations but come out unscathed as he did by being acquitted on five charges in 2021. It shows that he will fight against social injustice.

Kyle, a humanitarian and leader, will be known for his writing. He will get into politics and rise in influence. Around the age of 30 to 40, Kyle will become well-known for his positive changes to the world.

CHAPTER 10

PRESIDENTIAL RACE 2024

President Joe Biden will go down in history books as the worst president ever. He's been gaslighting us with fear and lies since his election. Most of the time he and his wife Jill are at their home in Delaware and do not reside at the White House. I don't foresee Biden lasting in office until 2024, and he may not last until the end of 2022. Now the idiot media that once supported him, are berating him and his rating has dropped lower than Trump when he left office. Biden never spoke at a rally before being elected to explain his policies, and still, people voted for him. Now MSNBC says he's too old and doesn't seem to be in charge.

Recently, a Facebook follower jumped on my page and claimed Joe Biden has united Americans as he promised during his presidential campaign. How can this woman be so disconnected from what is going on in our country? Biden's ratings are dropping faster than you can blink an eye.

Stadium attendees for football games in 2021 chanted in unison, "F**k Biden." If that's uniting the American people, I must be living in a parallel world other than the Facebook follower. People are disappointed in Biden and his COVID vaccine mandates that haven't worked and how he has criticized the unvaccinated as "white supremacists" and as those spreading COVID, which is a lie.

Joe Biden was asked if he will run for re-election in 2024 at the age of 82, and he said a definite yes, but it won't happen. Joe Biden has made it clear he has cognitive issues with his constant faux pas throughout the year. He has continued to refer to vice president Kamala Harris as President Harris, and recently said it was 2020, instead of 2022. Biden had a health check-up for 2022. Where is his cognitive test? That's on American minds. It's clear, from his often strange or befuddled behavior, that something isn't right with him and that's why 59 percent of voters want him to take a cognitive test and release the results, according to a new McLaughlin & Associates survey published in the Washington Examiner.

The White House released the results of his first official physical examination but omitted any reference to Biden's mental faculties.

Biden's stiff gait has been observed, and gait disorders, especially stiffer, shortened, and more asymmetric strides, as Biden exhibits, are often linked to dementia, which is why Dr. Marc Siegel, a clinical professor of medicine at NYU Langone Medical Center, told Fox News he is concerned Biden health report left out crucial information.

Another emotion Biden often exhibits is anger. Alzheimer's patients get frustrated and show anger at little things. If that is true, Biden's wife, Jill, and everyone around him knows he has this horrible disease. They wanted a puppet president to control, but who are "they."

Former President Obama might be Biden's controller or even Bernie Sanders, a Socialist. If you think back to 2020, it took Obama a long time to endorse Biden for the presidential election. Obama supposedly cautioned another Democrat 'not to underestimate Joe's ability to f**k things up.'

How can we forget that Joe Biden's son, Hunter Biden, was involved with drugs, human trafficking, and child exploitation?

His revealing laptop tells the story, but the FBI refused to release it or convict Hunter.

Biden's laptop has been at the center of a confusing and ongoing scandal since its existence was first revealed in a controversial *New York Post* article last October 14. Steve Bannon, a former top adviser to Trump known for strategically planting stories and rumors in the press, initially tipped the existence of the laptop to the *Post* in September 2020. According to the *Post*, the laptop was dropped off at a repair shop, the owner of which reported the contents to the FBI. (In a recent interview given to promote his new book, Hunter Biden claimed he didn't know whether or not the laptop was his.)

The laptop allegedly contained "smoking-gun" emails between Ukrainian businessman Vadym Pozharskyi, an executive at the energy company Burisma, and Biden, who was paid as much as $50,000 a month to advise the company on the strength of his family name. In an email revealed by the *Post*, Pozharskyi thanked Biden for introducing him to his father, the then-vice president, whom Republicans claimed had used his office to pressure Ukrainian officials into firing a top prosecutor allegedly investigating Burisma. As was widely reported, Vice-President Biden did the opposite and pressured the Ukrainian government to oust the prosecutor for corruption. The story initiated a storm of conspiracy theories from QAnon supporters, who latched on to claims that there was content on the hard drive depicting Hunter Biden smoking crack and engaging in sexual acts with underage girls.

No one would have voted for a President if they had known about his dementia or Alzheimer's disease. Yet, the people around him allowed it. Remember how seldom Biden spoke at rallies around the country, unlike President Trump who drew huge crowds before the November 4, 2021 election. At times, Biden didn't know what state of the union he was in that's because he was in a state of confusion! It was probably the 'state of confusion' as some have suggested.

Since Biden was elected inflation is nearly 8%, gas prices have risen, and unemployment is at the highest it's been in years with people quitting due to the COVID vaccine mandates or refusing to go back to work. Small businesses have vanished due to COVID mandates. Children had lost nearly two years in education and in most schools CRT (Critical Race Theory) is being taught in schools. CRT is an intellectual approach to looking at the United States society with a belief that racism is at the core of its laws and institutions. There are videos of children crying to their parents that they were the wrong skin color, or their parents are "white supremacists or racist."

Biden has allowed at least 2 million illegals to cross over the Texas, Arizona, and California borders from Mexico in the past two years, entering our country without COVID vaccines and without being vetted. Large numbers of adults and even children have been secretly flown to cities in the middle of the night and then bused elsewhere. Many of the migrants, entering the U.S. illegally, are drug cartels, terrorists, sex offenders, murders, and hardened criminals. But Joe and the Democrat party don't care. They only want to ensure Democrats remain in office indefinitely by allowing all illegal migrants to vote—no identification or U.S. citizenship needed.

In Hungary, they have stopped illegals from crossing into their country with electric and barbed wire fences and placing troops there to stop the invaders. Now, Biden has torn down a lot of Trump's huge walls on the Texas border, and it's going to sell most of it for pennies on the dollar.

Remember how Joe deserted thousands of Afghanistan people who worked for the United States, and the Afghan military and their families in Afghanistan. On August 18, President Biden said there were citizens left in Afghanistan who wanted to leave, and "we're gonna stay to get them all out." But that's not what happened when the last U.S. soldier departed the country. Biden broke his promise. God knows if those people are still alive or were killed by the Taliban. The White House claims there are 100 to 200 people left behind, but other sources say there are more.

This was a huge disgrace to our country and our military who fought in Afghanistan for years.

When we suddenly pulled out of Afghanistan, the U.S. military likely abandoned tens of millions of dollars' worth of aircraft, armored vehicles, and sophisticated defensive systems in the rush to leave the airport in Kabul safely. Some of the military armor was inoperable, but the Taliban didn't waste any time proving that most of it did work in their videos.

On January 11, 2022, Biden announced the U.S. is donating

approximately $308 million in humanitarian aid to Afghanistan and will also contribute additional COVID-19 vaccine doses, according to a White House spokesperson. Where do you think that money will go? That's right—to the corrupt Taliban terrorists.

Biden has spent money like water running through his hands since 2020. The Biden administration released $350 billion in COVID-19 relief funding for state and local governments in 2021. Biden's 1.75 trillion dollars infrastructure bill was finally passed, but it's not for our deteriorating bridges and roads, but mostly for the Democrat's special interest agendas.

U.S. oil production was shut down after Biden was elected and thousands of oil workers became unemployed. Now 85% of crude oil imports come from Canada, Saudi Arabia, Mexico, Venezuela, and Columbia. Biden has made it his job to undo everything Trump did as President.

Biden has created a division between the vaccinated and the unvaccinated by demonizing the unvaccinated for all the new cases of Omicron, but the truth is it's not just the unvaccinated but a great number of vaccinated who are having breakthrough cases. Most businesses, Federal employees, pilots, and other businesses have been forced to get the vaccines or get fired for refusing a vaccine that still hasn't been tested enough. Pfizer and other vaccines have shown horrible side effects such as blood clotting.

Don't expect Kamala Harris to enter the 2024 race—she'll never make it past first base. Most of her staff has walked out and most voters dislike her. The only way she's staying in office is if Biden died and she became President and that's a terrifying thought.

Donald Trump and 2024

While Trump was President, he stopped illegals from flooding our borders, unemployment was at an all-time low, gasoline prices were around $2.49/gal., the U.S. had our own oil reserves, the stock market rose strongly during Trump's term, with the S&P 500 up over 50% since the November 2016 election, more than in the four years following Democrat Barack Obama's first election win in 2008. Trump seemed to have an amicable relationship with Russian leader Putin and North Korean leader Kim Jong-un, unlike Biden who can't get along with Russia and

Kim Jong-un.

People still love Trump because we had a better life before Biden was elected and COVID hit. But will voters forgive him for any of his past transgressions—such as hanging out with sex trafficker Jeffrey Epstein, who trafficked underage girls? Trump took at least eight trips on Jeffrey Epstein's "Lolita Express" private plane, according to newly released flight logs during December 2021. Trump was one of several elite passengers on the sex-predator financier's private jet. The 118 pages of flight logs released, also list nine trips by former President Bill Clinton, as well as lawyer Alan Dershowitz, former U.S. Senator George Mitchell, and Prince Andrew.

Trump's ego has never been his amigo, and that will never change. 2024 is still over two years away, and much can change in the timeline.

A vision seven months before Trump won the 2016 election, showed me that he would take the presidential oath (my prediction is still on the Newsmax website). I was shown he would be re-elected in 2021, but there were indications that ballot harvesting and other shenanigans took place in certain states to elect Biden. Some want to debate this, but what is done is done.

On January 6, 2021, Trump went back to the White House and it is believed that his children, Ivanka Trump and Donald Trump Jr., tried to persuade him to make a statement to stop what was going on as people pushed into the Capitol building. Even if he had tried to stop it, who would have listened to his plea to stop.

Born on June 14, 1946, Donald Trump is a Gemini, with Leo rising, Mars in Leo, and Pluto in Leo. Geminis are often known as fast talkers, social, and sometimes deceptive. His rising sign in Leo gives him the ego and his need to be in the spotlight at all times. He will be 78-years-old in 2024.

Biden and the Democratic Congress want to stop him from being elected. They tried twice to impeach him and failed. The Democratic Congress, Pelosi, and her minion haven't given up. There are calling everyone in Trump's circle including his children, to testify about January 6, even if they weren't in D.C. that day.

Recently, Trump was heckled in Dallas, Texas for confirming he had received his COVID-19 booster shot along with former

Fox News host Bill O'Reilly. He supports inoculations. However, he noted that the vaccine had saved lives, but he said he was against President Biden's vaccine mandate. He said, "But the mandates, they should not be—and they are trying to enforce these mandates, and it's so bad for people and our country."

Trump hasn't officially said he will run in 2024 but has hinted at it. By all indications, I'd say a definite yes, he will run. The tarot card read leadership upside down which I interpret to mean he won't be elected in 2024. But, I could be wrong because his personal year in 2024, is number 1, a year of new beginnings, initiatives, and decisions to be made for the future.

Hillary Clinton for President?

Hillary Clinton has never healed over losing to Trump in 2016, even crying about it during a televised interview. Democrats are already suggesting that Hillary will be the only one suitable for running against any Republican in 2024. Could it be a rematch between Clinton and Trump? It could happen, but do you really want it to happen again?

Hillary is a Scorpio, born October 26, 1947, and will be 77 years old in 2024. As a Scorpio, she can sting if slighted with her temper.

I have often referred to the book, *Transformation of America,* by Cathy O'Brien. This is the documented autobiography of a victim of government mind control. O'Brien was a recovered survivor of the CIA's (Central Intelligence Agency) MK-Ultra Project Monarch mind control operation as a child. She was sexually abused, and people named in her book included Bill and Hillary Clinton, former Vice President Dick Cheney, and former President George H.W. Bush. She wrote, "My introduction to Cheney was in the summer of 1975 at his Greybull, Wyoming hunting lodge where he was indulging in his favorite sport of human hunting. This military training exercise, referred to as *A Most Dangerous Game*, was Cheney's sport of choice along with his hunting buddies George Bush, Sr., and Bill Clinton as detailed in my testimony for Congress in *Trance Formation of America.*

Here is an excerpt from O'Brien's book, *Trance Formation of America.*

"Dick Cheney had an apparent addiction to the 'thrill of the sport'. He appeared obsessed with playing A Most Dangerous

Game as a means of traumatizing mind-control victims, as well as to satisfy his own perverse sexual kinks."

"My introduction to the game occurred upon arrival at the hunting lodge near Greybull, Wyoming, and it physically and psychologically devastated me.

"I was sufficiently traumatized for Cheney's programming as I stood naked in his hunting lodge office after being hunted down and caught.

"Cheney was talking as he paced around me, 'I could stuff you and mount you like a jackalope and call you a two-legged dear [sic]. Or I could stuff you with this (he unzipped his pants...) right down your throat, and then mount you. Which do you prefer?

"Blood and sweat became mixed with the dirt on my body and slid like mud down my legs and shoulder. I throbbed with exhaustion and pain as I stood unable to think to answer such a question.

"'Make up your mind,' Cheney coaxed. Unable to speak, I remained silent. 'You don't get a choice, anyway, I make up your mind for you. That's why you're here. For me to make you a' mind, and make you mine/mind. You lost your mind a long time ago.

"Now I'm going to give you one. Just like the Wizard (of Oz) gave Scarecrow a brain, the Yellow Brick Road led you here to me. You've 'come such a long, long way' for your brain, and I will give you one.

"The blood reached my shoes and caught my attention. Had I been further along in my programming, 1 perhaps would never have noticed such a thing or had the capability to think to wipe it away.

"But so far, I had only been to MacDill and Disney World for government/military programming. At last, when I could speak, I begged, 'If you don't mind, can I please use your bathroom?'

"Cheney's face turned red with rage. He was on me in an instant, slamming my back into the wall with one arm across my chest and his hand on my throat, choking me while applying pressure to the carotid artery in my neck with his thumb.

"His eyes bulged, and he spit as he growled, 'If you don't mind me, I will kill you. I could kill you—kill you with my bare hands. You're not the first and you won't be the last. I'll kill you any time I goddamn well please.'

"He [Cheney] flung me on the cot-type bed that was behind me. There he finished taking his rage out on me sexually."

Cathy O'Brien also accused Hillary Clinton of rape in graphic detail. Everyone, except the general public, seems to know that Hillary prefers women. Another interesting observation there is a photo circulating the internet that shows sex trafficker and pedophile Jeffery Epstein and his associate girlfriend, Ghislaine Maxwell, in attendance at Bill and Hillary's daughter, Chelsea Clinton's wedding in 2010.

If you think Hillary and Bill Clinton are normal people, you'd better think again. As George Bush would have said, they are "evil doers," a term he often used while President. With former President Bill Clinton potentially being implicated in the crimes committed on Epstein's island of horrors, many are suggesting the suicide was just another Clinton coverup.

The Clinton murder theory is not without merit when you consider the number of mysterious deaths associated with the Clintons. The Clinton mafia "Kill List" as it's often referred to has been circulating the internet for years, and there have been many attempts to debunk it. However, as time goes by and the list grows even bigger, we have to agree that 27 deaths connected to the Clinton deaths are beyond coincidence. I can guarantee the "Rabbit Hole" goes deeper than you can imagine.

Here is the list of people who died around the Clintons:

1- James McDougal – Clinton's convicted Whitewater partner died of an apparent heart attack, while in solitary confinement. He was a key witness in Ken Starr's investigation.

2 – Mary Mahoney – A former White House intern was murdered in July 1997 at a Starbucks Coffee Shop in Georgetown .. The murder ...happened just after she was to go public w:th her story of sexual harassment in the White House.

3 – Vince Foster – Former White House counselor, and colleague of Hillary Clinton at Little Rock's Rose Law firm. Died of a gunshot wound to the head, ruled a suicide.

4 – Ron Brown – Secretary of Commerce and former DNC Chairman. Reported to have died by impact in a plane crash. A pathologist close to the investigation reported that there was a hole in the top of Brown's skull resembling a gunshot wound. At the time of his death, Brown was being investigated and spoke publicly of his willingness to cut a deal with prosecutors. The rest of the people on the plane also died. A few days later, the Air Traffic controller committed suicide.

5 – C. Victor Raiser, II – Raiser, a major player in the Clinton fundraising organization died in a private plane crash in July 1992.

6 – Paul Tulley – Democratic National Committee Political Director found dead in a hotel room in Little Rock, in September 1992. Described by Clinton as a "dear friend and trusted advisor".24 – Johnny Lawhorn

7 – Ed Willey – Clinton fundraiser, found dead in November 1993 deep in the woods in VA of a gunshot wound to the head. Ruled a suicide. Ed Willey died on the same day his wife Kathleen Willey claimed Bill Clinton groped her in the oval office in the White House. Ed Willey was involved in several Clinton fundraising events.

8 – Jerry Parks – Head of Clinton's gubernatorial security team in Little Rock .. Gunned down in his car at a deserted intersection outside Little Rock Park's son said his father was building a dossier on Clinton He allegedly threatened to reveal this information. After he died the files were mysteriously removed from his house.

9 – James Bunch – Died from a gunshot suicide. It was reported that he had a "Black Book" of people which contained names of influential people who visited prostitutes in Texas and Arkansas.

10 – James Wilson – Was found dead in May 1993 from an apparent hanging suicide. He was reported to have ties to Whitewater.

11 – Kathy Ferguson – Ex-wife of Arkansas Trooper Danny Ferguson, was found dead in May 1994, in her living room with a gunshot to her head. It was ruled a suicide even though there were several packed suitcases as if she were going somewhere. Danny Ferguson was a co-defendant along with Bill Clinton in the Paula Jones lawsuit Kathy Ferguson was a possible corroborating witness for Paula Jones.

12 – Bill Shelton – Arkansas State Trooper and fiancée of Kathy Ferguson. Critical of the suicide ruling of his fiancée, he was found dead in June 1994 of a gunshot wound also ruled a suicide at the grave site of his fiancée.

13 – Gandy Baugh – Attorney for Clinton's friend Dan Lassater, died by jumping out a window of a tall building in January 1994. His client was a convicted drug distributor.

12 – Bill Shelton – Arkansas State Trooper and fiancée of Kathy Ferguson. Critical of the suicide ruling of his fiancée, he was found dead in June 1994 of a gunshot wound also ruled a suicide at the grave site of his fiancée.

13 – Gandy Baugh – Attorney for Clinton's friend Dan Lassater, died by jumping out a window of a tall building in January 1994. His client was a convicted drug distributor.

14 – Florence Martin – Accountant & sub-contractor for the CIA, was related to the Florence **Martine** Barry Seal, Mena, Arkansas, airport drug smuggling case. He died of three gunshot wounds.

15 – Suzanne Coleman – Reportedly had an affair with Clinton when he was Arkansas Attorney General. Died of a gunshot wound to the back of the head, ruled a suicide. Was pregnant at the time of her death.

16 – Paula Grober – Clinton's speech interpreter for the deaf from 1978 until her death on December 9, 1992. She died in a one-car accident.

17 – Danny Casolaro – Investigative reporter, investigating

Mena Airport and Arkansas Development Finance Authority. He slit his wrists, apparently, in the middle of his investigation.

18 – Paul Wilcher – Attorney investigating corruption at Mena Airport with Casolaro and the 1980 "October Surprise" was found dead on a toilet on June 22, 1993, in his Washington DC apartment had delivered a report to Janet Reno 3 weeks before his death.

19 – Jon Parnell Walker – Whitewater investigator for Resolution Trust Corp. Jumped to his death from his Arlington, Virginia apartment balcony on August 15, 1993. He was investigating the Morgan Guaranty scandal.

20 – Barbara Wise – Commerce Department staffer. Worked closely with Ron Brown and John Huang. Cause of death: Unknown. Died November 29, 1996. Her bruised, naked body was found locked in her office at the Department of Commerce.

21 – Charles Meissner – Assistant Secretary of Commerce who gave John Huang special security clearance, died shortly thereafter in a small plane crash.

22 – Dr. Stanley Heard – Chairman of the National Chiropractic Health Care Advisory Committee died with his attorney Steve Dickson in a small plane crash. Dr. Heard, in addition to serving on Clinton's advisory council personally treated Clinton's mother, stepfather, and brother.

23 – Barry Seal – Drug running TWA pilot out of Mena Arkansas, death was no accident.

24 – Johnny Lawhorn, Jr. – Mechanic, found a check made out to Bill Clinton in the trunk of a car left at his repair shop. He was found dead after his car had hit a utility pole.

25 – Stanley Huggins – Investigated Madison Guaranty. His death was a purported suicide and his report was never released.

26 – Hershell Friday – Attorney and Clinton fundraiser died March 1, 1994, when his plane exploded.

27 – Kevin Ives & Don Henry – Known as "The boys on the track" case. Reports say the boys may have stumbled upon the Mena Arkansas airport drug operation. A controversial case, the initial report of death said, due to falling asleep on railroad tracks. Later reports claim the 2 boys had been slain before being placed on the tracks. Many linked to the case died before their testimony could come before a Grand Jury.

The names listed below are the bodyguards who worked for the Clintons who also died under mysterious circumstances:

1 - Major William S. Barkley, Jr.
2 – Captain Scott J . Reynolds
3 – Sgt. Brian Hanley
4 – Sgt. Tim Sabel
5 – Major General William Robertson
6 – Col. William Densberger
7 – Col. Robert Kelly
8 – Spec. Gary Rhodes
9 – Steve Willis
10 – Robert Williams
11 – Conway LeBleu
12 – Todd McKeehan

James Allard researched the list of the dead. He has been with Oye Alternative News from the start, with extensive knowledge across a wide range of subjects his work is diverse.

Can you say Clinton mafia? It is surprising Trump hasn't met with a similar fate. Fox host Tucker Carlson remarked on his January 12, 2022 television talk show that Hillary didn't kill Epstein. He was joking but he seemed to imply that Hillary was also involved with Epstein's sexual slave house with underage girls for prostitution. I predict that Epstein's girlfriend, Ghislaine will meet with a similar fate as Epstein—dead in prison by what will look like suicide.

These people are dark, and they don't understand the concept of real compassionate love. With them, it's about control and power. Our world is full of what you might call Satanists and antichrists, heartless, soulless humans.

The question you all want to know is will Hillary Clinton run again. I can see it, but she will never be elected president.

Florida Governor Ron DeSantis
Ron DeSantis, a Virgo, was born on September 14, 1978, in Jacksonville, Florida, and will turn 46 years old in 2024. DeSantis is a Republican politician and an attorney serving as the 46th governor of Florida since 2019.

DeSantis served in the Navy as a Lieutenant in 2006 as an attorney. In 2007, DeSantis reported to the Naval Special Warfare Command Group in Coronado, California, where he was assigned to SEAL Team One and deployed to Iraq. He returned to the United States in April 2008 and was reassigned to the Naval Region Southeast Legal Service.

The two are among the most popular Republican figures in the country, and with Trump eyeing another presidential run in 2024, many political pundits believe he is irritated by DeSantis' interest in running against him and his growing popularity. The adviser claimed McConnell sees DeSantis as a 'lesser of two evils' and a way to irritate Trump.

Although the news has claimed Trump and DeSantis are at odds with each other, Trump recently said there is not truth to the rumors. It's all fake news. DeSantis would be an intimidating 2024 candidate for Trump should Trump run. Dan Eberhart, a Republican donor, told the Times, "He's Trump but a little smarter, more disciplined and brusque, without being too brusque."

Trump in October 2021 said he would easily 'beat him (DeSantis).' "If I faced him, I'd beat him like I would beat everyone else," he said at the time.

Already the Democrats are doing everything to berate him for handling COVID-19 in Florida. Recently, monoclonal treatment centers were banned in Florida by the FDA. That's insane.

Florida's governor Ron DeSantis is up for re-election in 2022, and I foresee him having a big win. I foresee a very strange pairing in 2024 between Governor DeSantis against Democratic Senator Joe Machin, who dances to his own tune and not necessarily to what Congress wants. Both are Virgos, both are Italian Catholics, both are family men and both appear to be working for American citizens.

Democrat Senator Joe Machin
Joe Machin, a Virgo, was born on August 24, 1947, in a small

coal-mining town of West Virginia in a large family. His father was Italian. The name Machin is derived from the Italian name Manchini. Joe Machin dances to his own tune and doesn't follow what the other Democrats dictate. He served as 34th governor of West Virginia from 2005 to 2010. He refers to himself as a "centrist, moderate, conservative Democrat" and is usually cities as the most conservative Democrat in the Senate. Machin is known for his bipartisanship in working with Republicans on issues such as abortion, immigration, energy, and gun control. Machine said he would not vote on Biden's $2 trillion Build Back Better Act and climate policy. Joe Machin will be 77-years-old in 2024.

Like Florida's Governor DeSantis, Machin is an Italian, Catholic, and a Virgo, and his Personal Year numerological vibration for 2024 is number 4, the same as DeSantis. Odd coincidence, or is it? The number 4 vibration relates to success. I foresee that Democrat Joe Machin and Republican Ron DeSantis will run against each other in 2024. They have karma together, but it looks like DeSantis will have the edge over Machin.

Mike Pence

Mike Pence has always pictured himself as President, but after January 6. Former Vice President Mike Pence most forceful rejection came when he didn't support Trump's belief the 2020 election was rigged. However, Pence has declined to directly criticize Trump by name or assign him any blame for inciting the Capitol attack on January 6.

Pence speaking at the Ronald Reagan Presidential Library in Simi Valley, California last year, insisted he was not constitutionally empowered to reverse the election results when he presided over the counting of electoral votes in Congress in January. Trump had urged him to do that in the hours before MAGA supporters stormed the Capitol building. Pence said, "But the Constitution provides the vice president with no such authority before the joint session of Congress. And the truth is, there's almost no idea more un-American than the notion that any one person could choose the American president."

Mike Pence, a Gemini like Trump, was born on June 7, 1959, and will be 65-years-old in 2024. His personal vibration number in 2024 will be number 3 which denotes travel, expansion, and self-expression. Pence will probably throw his hat into the Presidential race, but won't go far.

Democrats who may run in 2024

Michelle Obama, Kamala Harris, and Elizabeth Warren don't stand a chance if they plan to run. Liz Cheney is just as corrupt as her father, former Vice President Dick Cheney. Remember, the apple doesn't fall far from the tree. She believes that she can win the 2024 Presidential election, but it will never happen.

CHAPTER 11

THE WAR ON ASCENSION

James Gilliland is a best-selling author, internationally known lecturer, minister, a near-death experiencer, and ET contactee. He is the owner of the ECETI Ranch in Southwestern Washington State where people come to experience Enlightened Contact with Multi-Dimensional beings. He posted this message on his Facebook page and asked that his message be shared freely.

The War on Ascension, Message for Humanity

It is said we are not fighting a war of flesh and bones but a war against principalities and spirit. This is the big picture unless factored in nothing else makes sense. To be enlightened is to be in knowledge of, all of it, both sides of the coin the agenda's goals, and the modus operandi of the light and dark. The light side is all about empowerment, service to others, operating under universal law which in its simplest form is Universal Peace, Brother/Sisterly Love, Individual Freedom, and Prosperity for All. There are multidimensional legions of beings operating under universal law in service to Humanity and the Earth as well as the Creator in all Creation. Many of these beings are spiritually and technologically advanced off worlders as well as those who ascended from Earth known as Ascended Masters, Angelic Guides Male, and Female.

Just as there is a light side there is a dark side. There are those off worlders who are technologically advanced yet spiritually backward, in service to self often referred to but not limited to greys and reptilians, the Grey Alliance. There are masters of the dark, demons, disfigured malevolent people trapped in the astral levels or 4thdimension some call the lower 4th density. Most are there due to extreme attachment, confusion, or a history of breaking the Universal Law.

Satanic/Luciferian groups work with these dark energies to influence and gain power over others and wealth regardless of any negative impact or how it affects humanity and the Earth. Unfortunately, these people assume authority beyond what is given and gravitate to positions of power and influence. From these positions, they prey on the ignorant and less fortunate. They are replete within the political, religious, and business institutions including the movie and music industry. They own and control the mainstream and social media designed to socially engineer the people to meet their agendas. This will all be made known. It is said a man's/woman's character is established by their actions. Watch their actions off stage out of the public eye. The facades and masks are coming down. The truth will no longer be suppressed.

The war on ascension is a war on evolving consciousness. It is a war on your body, your mind, and your spirit. The war on the body has several fronts. They have polluted the air with manufacturing and energy-generating waste, "chemtrails and geoengineering". They pollute the water with a myriad of toxic, carcinogenic chemicals, "fluoride". They have polluted your food with toxic additives and preservatives. The pollution and destruction of the land as well to keep you enslaved through dependency, "oil, coal and nuclear" fit into these categories. We have had free energy, anti/counter gravity, and interplanetary travel since the early '60s. Where is it? Would that free the people, clean up the environment?

It is as if these tyrants are at war with Creation in their unbridled greed and they are at that because the darkness they serve demands it. Now they are going after your DNA. Why would they go after your DNA? Did you know the name YHWH is written or coded into your DNA? Man/Woman are created in the same image and likeness of God/Creator/Great Spirit. You have the DNA of the Gods. You also have the spark that can be ignited into the full flame, the one consciousness that encompasses all consciousness on all planes and dimensions throughout the universe. Knowing and owning this is their greatest fear. Those trying to alter your DNA are working against God's plan, doing the work of the dark forces, pure and simple. Your DNA is being activated in the process known as ascension. The whole planet is ascending.

What happens when one ascends or becomes enlightened? They cannot be controlled. What happens to the tyrants when the people and the Earth ascend? Game over. They are hell-bent literally on stopping ascension.

There are those who feed off the suppression, pain, and suffering without which their world would no longer exist. These are the forces and motives behind the enslavement, pain, and suffering throughout history and not just Earth history. It is a war between God and Evil and it is multidimensional. Before the condescending spiritual egos pop up and say you are polarizing, creating fear and division going biblical on us these my friends are one of many psyops created within the spiritual community to allow the dark side to function unchallenged. A half-truth created and perpetuated by the dark side.

Those aligned with the dark side are agenda and profit-driven. Those who work for the light are heart and service-driven. It matters not what culture, religion, gender, or belief. The dark hearts have moved into positions of power, they control the money, the mainstream and social media, the medical industry, and those agencies charged with oversight. The W.H.O, the C.D.C., and the F.D.A. are funded by the vaccine makers, mainly the Gates Foundation, the CCP, the Chinese Communist Party, and other global elites. These agencies are revolving doors between big pharma and the agencies. It recently came to light there were massive bribes by the major vaccine companies to officials in these agencies as well as politicians etc. to promote, even mandate the vaccines. The main funders of these integrity-challenged agencies funded the gain of function bioweapons, known as Covid-19, and the mysterious nonverifiable variants all waiting in line to be released to perpetuate their profit and agendas. This corruption includes many of the enforcement agencies, alphabet agencies, and even some high-level officials in the military who have all abandoned their oaths. The Hippocratic oath and the oath to serve God and country, protect the people and the Constitution.

The White Hats are those within the political, religious, medical, business institutions and agencies who remember and abide by their oaths. The lines are being drawn, choices are being made and those choices will have consequences determining one's future.

Little hint, God wins. Another little hint when you pass this plane you will have a light review where you will experience and feel all the pain and suffering and loss inflicted on others. This is unavoidable.

Action/Reaction or Karma is being accelerated, no rock will be left unturned, all the iniquities will be shouted from the rooftops, the wheat is being separated from the chaff. Sound familiar? Some call it the Great Awakening. Others call it ascension. This is not spiritual mumbo jumbo or woo-woo. It is prophecy and science coming together. The Schumann Frequency is off the scale with one massive influx of energy after the other. C.M.E.s coronal mass ejections or solar flares are also on the increase. This is exponentially getting stronger. Our solar system is going through a highly energized position in space and the electromagnetic light spectrum is increasing with more bands being added. There is also a massive influx of consciousness and energy due to the higher dimensional beings adding their consciousness and energy to the collective consciousness and energy of Earth. Creator has given its best for these times—the pain, suffering, and loss inflicted on others.

This is unavoidable.

Imagine the impact that will have on this civilization socially, energetically, physically right down to the atomic structure, your very DNA. Did you know cosmic energies create changes in your DNA and cosmic energies according to NASA have increased exponentially? This is the Creator at work. All the Suns are connected to a Great Central Sun, the source of what is happening is beyond this solar system, beyond this dimension. Most cannot even comprehend what is unfolding.

When you understand what is in the experimental gene therapy, the operating system injected into you they call a vaccine, what it does to your DNA, how it disconnects you spiritually, can be manipulated externally with 5G putting your life on a timer to meet their population reduction guidelines you will understand the real agenda and who is behind it. It is anti-Christ consciousness, anti-life. It is a war on ascension by those who want total domination over every aspect of your life. Billionaire eugenicists, Satanic/Luciferians void of compassion and empathy that sold their souls a long time ago for power and wealth. They are agenda and profit-driven regardless of the consequence to you, your families, and the Earth. This includes the crippling and death of millions, some of which have already happened. They have financed both sides of every war since Napoleon. For those who cannot comprehend this because it is so evil, that is what they are counting on. They are counting on the ignorance and denial of the masses as well the lack of impeccable integrity, infinite excuses for not doing what is right. The one thing the dark hearts did not factor in. The soul activation and awakening of the masses, divine intervention, and another plan the origin of which is on high beyond their perception. Ascension, The Great Awakening, The Spiritual Revolution no matter what you call it, it is here. It is time to find impeccable integrity within, honor your oaths, follow your heart and be of service to the Creator within all Creation, humanity, and the Earth. The winning side.

We are eternal souls and it is better to die free in integrity, in service to Creator and all Creation than to be a slave to the darkness. What you do now will not only determine your future in this life, but it will also determine where you go in the hereafter and the future of generations to come.

The law is on your side, Universal or God's Law. They are breaking Constitutional Law, The Nuremberg Codes, and the MA international code of ethics. They have broken their Hippocratic oaths and oaths to serve God and the Country protecting the Constitution and the People.

Government has but one function to preserve your rights and freedom, not violate them. Doing otherwise is sedition or treason. They have declared war on the very people they profess to serve. We have complied with systematic stolen authority that has become cancer on the back of the Republic. It is time for peaceful non-compliance with the illegal, unscientific, and harmful mandates that have destroyed our health and our economy which was always the end goal of the tyrants. It is time for critical thinking, time to do your own research, step away from social engineering, mainstream, and social media. It is time to stand in the truth, stand in our divinity, protect the next generation and hold those who are transgressing on those rights accountable. Another word for unlawful authority is tyranny. America was founded on freedom from tyranny. It is inherently against tyranny. Coming together and supporting each other in peaceful non-compliance is the answer. It cuts the legs off of tyranny. The beginning. By James Gilliland

The old people used to say that the trees, the rocks, the birds, and the animals used to talk. They had a voice, and today, as I realize it, they still have a voice. My people always say that you have to take care of them in order for you to continue on. If you don't, when they die off, you are going to die with them. —Spiritual Leader of the Western Shoshone Nation Corbin Harney (1920-2007)

CHAPTER 12

EARTH CHANGES

Something is happening inside our planet with mysterious booms heard worldwide for the past ten years, volcanoes erupting worldwide, powerful earthquakes increasing, and countless UFO orbs sightings witnessed in the past two years. Environmental indicators show certain ecological events that have been stable for the past half million years are changing rapidly within the last few decades. The ecological planetary disaster is looming over us, and this is a direct reflection of the state of human consciousness. The Thirteen Indigenous Grandmothers from around the world have been told by spiritual beings that we have a symbiotic relationship with Earth, and if wars stopped and we started honoring Earth, there will be fewer Earth changes taking place.

The outer world we live in is a mirror of the inner domain. We are the environment and must realize the power our thoughts have over our physical world.

Earth sizzled in 2021 as the sixth hottest year on record,

According to several newly released temperature measurements. scientists say that the increase in temperatures worldwide is a long-term trend that is accelerating. Gavin Schmidt, the climate scientist who heads NASA's temperature team said, "the long-term trend is very, very clear. And it's because of us. And it's not going to go away until we stop increasing the amount of carbon dioxide in the atmosphere."

Because of the rise in temperatures, Earth's weather has become extreme and chaotic. Drought has hit the Southwest of the United States, California, and parts of the Northwest for years. These areas are greatly concerned about water. For instance, Las Vegas gets 90% of its water from the Colorado River which empties into Lake Mead. Lake Mead is currently at its lowest level in history, but Las Vegas and its casinos, and people who own swimming pools won't alter their way of life. They aren't even thinking about water running out.

Already extreme weather is affecting the entire Earth. I foresee devasting floods, in some areas, drought and wildfires will be in the news for 2022, and these fires will be sudden and without warning as the winds whip them into fire storms. People will have little warning to escape these fires like the one that swept through suburban areas between Denver and Boulder, Colorado on December 30, 2021. It was considered among the most destructive in the state's history, destroying almost 1,000 homes and forcing tens of thousands of residents to flee for their lives.

Tornadoes usually happen in spring, but not anymore. They will hit any time of the year and be bigger and more destructive than ever. On December 11, 2021, eighty people were killed by dozens of tornadoes tearing through Kentucky, Illinois, Missouri, Tennessee, and Arkansas.

Volcanoes

In the past couple of years, volcanoes have become more explosive and more devastating. There will be more mysterious booms in 2022, and a day or two after, a huge earthquake or volcanic eruption will take place. Big noises will come from Mother Earth as a warning. There will be volcanoes erupting and some exploding that have been dormant for hundreds of years.

Between 2008 and 2018, Kilauea on the Island of Hawaii became active. It erupted almost continuously from vents on its eastern rift zone, causing property damage and destroying the towns of Kalapana and Kaimu, including its renowned black sand beach. The volcano's last eruption was on December 20, 2020.

On March 19, 2021, the Icelandic volcano Fagradalsfjall on the Reykjanes peninsula suddenly erupted when an eruptive fissure opened in the Geldingadalir valleys. It had been quiet for over six thousand years and was the first active volcano in the Reykjanes area for 800 years. The volcanic episode began three weeks before with intense earthquakes, the strongest registering 5.7 on the Richter Scale. In the following weeks, there were more than 40,000 earthquakes, mostly unfelt. The volcano finally quieted down on September 18, 2021.

Between 2008 and 2018, Kilauea on the Island of Hawaii became active. It erupted almost continuously from vents on its eastern rift zone, causing property damage and destroying the towns of Kalapana and Kaimu, including its renowned black sand beach.

On Christmas Day, December 25, 2021, the Cumbre Vieja volcano on the island of La Palma in the Canary Islands fell silent in the Canary Islands before causing massive destruction on the island, causing 7,000 people to evacuate, destroying over 3,000 buildings, and forming a new peninsula. The La Palma volcano lasted 91 days, erupting spectacularly, and then suddenly stopped in the new year. It's not dormant. More and more volcanoes are erupting.

Volcanoes will be erupting everywhere. There will be new volcanoes. Tsunamis will be taking place in the South Pacific as other volcanoes awaken.

Since Cumbre Vieja is silent now, another volcano awakened on January 15, 2022—an underwater volcano known as Tonga-Hunga Ha'apai exploded without warning. It was so powerful it was recorded around the world and triggered a tsunami that flooded Pacific coastlines from Japan to the western United States. Satellite images showed the long, rumbling eruption spewing ash and smoke in the air with a thunderous roar.

Mother Earth is going to show us just how fierce she can get with powerful tsunamis, volcanic eruptions, and destructive earthquakes in 2022.

In 2022, there will be huge volcanic eruptions on land and undersea causing major destruction. Watch the areas of the

South Pacific, Japan, Hawaii, Alaska Aleutian Islands, New Zealand, and possibly the Northwest of the United State.

Earthquakes
There will be earthquakes in places that are not known for earthquakes, and powerful earthquakes are large enough to generate tsunamis. The year 2021 was an exceptionally active period for global seismicity, with 19 major earthquakes, three of them registered over 8.0 magnitude and seventeen earthquakes registered 7.0 magnitude or higher, the most seismically active since 2007. Areas of concern in 2022: the New Madrid Seismic Zone this year that stretches from the southwest from New Madrid, Missouri, the West Coast from Oregon to Washington State from the Cascadia Subduction Zone, and the Tonga area in the South Pacific.

Tornadoes and Hurricanes
It will seem as if everything is upside down when it comes to storms and weather. A sudden plunge of temperatures in the summer and the winter with extreme cold, below zero in some areas, and heavy snowfall in February, but then a sudden warm-up in either late February or early March that will cause disastrous floods. Also, the sudden temperature changes will trigger tornadoes, bigger and stronger than we have seen before. Some will travel farther, up to 3 miles, destroying everything in their path.

Warming temperatures in the Atlantic and Pacific oceans will create larger hurricanes and more destructive ones. Seven hurricanes formed in 2021. Areas to watch—the Caribbean, the Gulf (Texas and Louisiana), and parts of Texas. Baja and parts of the Yucatan should be prepared for hurricanes in the Gulf and Pacific coastal areas.

Solar Eruptions and CMEs
The sun plays a major role in our lives and also the planet. Already the sun is producing some large flares and an X-Class flare was released in early January 2022.

Extreme Weather, Drought, and Wildfires

November 13, 2020, my book, *2021 Looking Into the Future,* was published. In the book, I predicted each year the weather will get fiercer from what scientists term climate change.

One thing I must reiterate in my books is that humans have not been good Earthkeepers. We litter, we pollute, we buy useless material things and usually toss them within a year. Our rivers, lakes, and oceans are polluted with plastics, syringes, sewage, oil, pesticides, and herbicides. Our water has become a giant toilet for humanity. Coral reefs are dying from what has been termed "bleaching" caused by global warming of our oceans, and from the dumping of toxins that enter the oceans from our rivers.

Our lack of love and compassion for our planet has created many of the horrible effects we see taking place worldwide. We have caused major destruction to our planet by removing oil, and precious minerals from the planet that are needed to balance the energy grid.

I have often thought that the chemtrail spraying from unmarked jets beginning in the late 1990s has contributed to global warming, but of course, we'll never know the truth until a pilot or a government official reveals the truth on their deathbed that chemtrails sprayed on the world to control us or lower our vibrational rate so that we would catch horrible new viruses (COVID-19?). What I sense is the chemtrail spraying was either to cover Planet X or to alter our DNA. Our governments have never been forthright with us with their ongoing black projects.

Human Migration

Huge migration of people everywhere trying to find peace from tyranny, mandates, horrible crime, and changing weather. People are leaving California, New York, and other places for several reasons—crime, homeless people, drugs, and extreme weather. They are tired of politicians that talk about change but do nothing or make things worse. Recently, California U-Haul reported that U-Haul trucks have vanished with huge numbers of people leaving the state. No one is moving into California.

Planet 9 or Planet X/Nibiru

Photographers have captured the drifting tail of Nibiru. According to Nancy Lieder's Zeta information, the Council of Worlds plans to allow a severe wobble on Earth to force the establishment to admit the reality of Planet X in our Solar System. In that such a temporary Severe Wobble would have to merge in with the Daily Earth Wobble, it is a tricky affair for the benign aliens arranging to fulfill the Council's edict. What this change does is ease the Daily Earth Wobble temporarily, while giving benign aliens the tools they need to affect a Severe Wobble. By suddenly allowing the magnetic flow surrounding Nibiru to change, allowing Nibiru's N Pole to drop and point again at the Earth, a mega wobble would be affected. This would be noticed by everyone on Earth, and the establishment would be scrambling to explain it. This temporarily Severe Wobble would be accompanied by dramatic visibility of Nibiru so that the usual excuses from NASA that the wobble was somehow from the Sun will not suffice.

CHAPTER 13

NESARA AND MED BEDS

In the mid-1990s, my long-time friend Janey told me about NESARA (National Economic Security and Recovery Act), and how Americans would have all debts wiped away, and the IRS would cease to exist. I told her, "No way will that ever happen." She wasn't going to hear any negative input about NESARA from me and held onto the belief and still believes it.

As of 2022, there are still people holding on to that fake information that our government would be that altruistic. Maybe in another reality but not this one.

NESARA was the brainchild of Harvey Francis Barnard who claimed that the proposals, which included replacing the income tax with a national sales tax, abolishing compound interest on secured loans, and returning to a bimetallic currency, would result in 0% inflation and create a more stable economy. The proposals were never introduced before Congress, but the NESARA legend lived on due to a woman named Shaini Candace Goodwin, doing business under the name of "Dove of Oneness."

She claimed the act was passed with additional provisions, but it was suppressed by George W. Bush's administration and the Supreme Court.

Goodwin eventually started her website, "Dove of Oneness" and began posting on her forums. It was later revealed that she was part of the cult group, *The Ramtha School of Enlightenment*.

Goodwin's website also claimed the NESARA bill floated around Congress before finally being passed by a secret session in March 2000 and signed by President Bill Clinton. It further claimed that the new law was to begin at 10 a.m. on September 11, 2001, but the computers and the data of the beneficiaries of the trillions of dollars of "Prosperity Fund" were destroyed on the second floor of the World Trade Center towers in New York City during the supposed terrorist attacks.

I doubt this happened, but it does make a nice story. Also, it was stated that an earlier gag order was issued by the Supreme Court which prohibited any official or private source from discussing it, under the penalty of death. She referred to the "White Knights" a group of high-ranking military officials who have since been struggling to have the law enacted despite opposition from President George W. Bush. Goodwin believed that Bush and his cronies orchestrated the September 11 attacks and the Iraq War as distractions from NESARA. She often claimed that Bush officials were attempting to hack into her site and prevent her from publicizing the law.

How many of you believe in Med Bed technology from the aliens and Nesara according to the UK psychic channeler named Christen Kwame on YouTube? Christen Kwame says on Instagram he is a singer-songwriter and Quantum/Shamanic Healer who books healing sessions. Perhaps he should stick to singing and songwriting.

Med Beds are supposed to be 3-d holographic healing technology that could happen in the future, but if this is alien technology, they aren't sharing it with us.

This is what is the mind control lunacy people buy into: They believe that med beds are real, they are already using them for damaged children who have been trafficked, and those in the military who have lost their limbs. Everyone will receive a med bed. President John F. Kennedy is still alive (he'd be 104- years old now!) and so is Jackie Kennedy, thanks to med bed technology! And the following people have been executed: Lady Gaga, Madonna, Tom Hanks, Julia Roberts, Jennifer Aniston, and Brad Pitt, and replaced with clones.

This lunacy is contagious and most of it comes from women who want to believe anything they watch on YouTube. Instead of thinking for themselves, they get wrapped up daily in YouTube videos, a horrible addiction they can't seem to stop. Just think what they could accomplish if they stayed off social media, and read a book, wrote a book, donated their time to charities, or took a class to improve themselves.

Prophecy 2022

CHAPTER 14

PROPHETS AND PSYCHICS

Humans have always sought seers, shamans, astrologers, and anyone who could peer into the future. Why are we so obsessed with the future if it is constantly changing and if the future holds dire events? Why would anyone want to know when their death approached? I would!

Michel de Nostre-Dame—Nostradamus was an astrologer and physician who was born at St. Remy de Provence on December 15, 1503. The hour of his birth was noon. Nostradamus loved looking into the future and predicting it in his book *The Centuries*, published in 1555. He predicted that King Henri II would die in a tournament against which he had been warned not to enter. A splinter from his opponent's lance shot through the French King's helmet, and penetrated an eye, causing him a lingering death. The quatrain in question is number 35 of the First Century, which reads:

The young lion will overcome the old one,
One field of battle in single combat:

In cage of gold his eyes will split.
Two raptures one, then to die, cruel death.

The quatrains were rhymed and short, but not actually poetry. They were ungrammatical, elliptical to the point, abstruse, and obscure. They included words not found in any French dictionary, refer to persons and places unknown, and are full of error, probably because of the early type-setters of the time. His prophecies were condemned by the papacy in 1781.

Nostradamus survived the plague that raged in the South of France during his lifetime and even cured people of it. How he brought about cures is a mystery. How did he combat the Black Death? How did he avoid contacting the disease himself?

Perhaps the great seer knew that he had a mission in life, and nothing could harm him until that mission was completed. Not even the Black Death could touch him.

The Apocalypse has been on human minds for eons—when will the Earth no longer exist and can we alter future events. It's a time when the Earth will vanish from a cataclysmic event.

Jeane Dixon, (1904-1997), was a famous psychic and astrology in the twentieth century. Her most famous prediction was the warning for President John F. Kennedy in 1963 that he would be assassinated. But like President Abraham Lincoln, he didn't listen to the warning. In the May 13, 1956 issue of Parade Magazine, Dixon predicted that the 1960 presidential election would be "dominated by labor and won by a Democrat" who would then go on to "be assassinated or die in office though not necessarily in his first term.

Dixon's predictions weren't always right. She had her misses. In 1972, her prediction of terrorist attacks in the United States in the wake of the Munich massacre spurred President Nixon to create a cabinet committee on counterterrorism. She was also one of several astrologers who advised Nancy Reagan during Ronald Reagan's presidency.

Dixon also predicted that before the end of the twentieth century, a pope would suffer bodily harm while another would be assassinated. Some believe that her prediction was about Pope Paul II who was nearly assassinated on May 13, 1981, while he was passing through the thousands of faithful gathered in St. Peter's Square, blessing the crowds from his open popemobile.

Pope Paul II claimed he believed the Virgin Mary had saved his life that day because May 13 was the month and day three children of Fatima, Portugal received apocalyptic visions and prophecies from the Virgin Mary from May 13, 1917, to October 13, 1917. Her visitations were always on the 13th day of the month and at solar noon.

Several pastors of churches proclaimed God had told them that Trump would be president again in 2021, and some proclaimed that Trump would somehow be restored to power. I wasn't one of those psychics. However, I did foresee him winning the November 2020 election, and I still believe that the election was not an honest one, especially now that Biden and the Democrats want to allow anyone, including illegals crossing our borders, the ability to vote in U.S. elections. How illegal is that? They are still trying to pass that voting law stating no ID is required for voting. Yet, we still all need an ID or passport to board a plane and get a driver's license.

No prophet or psychic is infallible. Why? Timelines are constantly changing, and the future is fluid and forming. Humans can be headed in one direction, and suddenly change their destiny. That's the beauty of free will. Some psychics, myself included, see a probable future or misinterpret the vision.

Edgar Cayce, (1878 -1949), was an American clairvoyant who channeled a higher consciousness, giving thousands of readings in a trance-like state. Usually, he correctly diagnosed illnesses for people from a distance or in his office. He gave predictions of the Earth shift coming in the twentieth or twenty-first century. But that still hasn't happened. Cayce also had skeptics and debunkers, but he did cure people of many illnesses during his lifetime that have been cataloged at the A.R.E. in Virginia, Beach, Virginia.

Nancy Lieder has been making Earth predictions since the 1990s, given to her by the Zeta aliens. She has stated that she was chosen to warn mankind about the brown dwarf or failed star called Nibiru or Planet X would sweep through the inner solar system in May 2003, causing Earth to undergo a physical pole shift, destroying most of humanity.

Nancy has been mostly accurate about the huge Earth changes taking place in the last fifteen years—earthquakes, volcanic eruptions, and extreme weather. She still maintains that Planet X/Nibiru is getting closer to our solar system and that's why things are on the uptick. She says the Earth will still shift poles.

Humans have some form of psychic ability. At some time in our lives, we've experienced a premonition of the future, either a gut feeling or a lucid dream that comes true. Before the events of September 11, 2001, some people worked in New York City at the Trade Tower buildings, and something either delayed them from going to work that day or they sensed they shouldn't go in, and their lives were saved. Coincidence? No, it wasn't their time to go.

Here's one such story from an unidentified man: "I worked two blocks away. My train would pull into the Trade Center around the time of the first attack every day. However, I wasn't there. The night before I had decided to take a personal day from work because September 11th was going to be a beautiful day and my husband wanted to take our one-year-old to the zoo.

On that day, 2,977 souls perished. All those people who overslept that day had no idea how it would change their lives forever.

Although I tell my client we have free will, our demise is preordained. We chose how we will leave this earthly plane. Some souls like to go it alone and others like to go in large groups. Accidents do happen from time to time, but souls have preselected their time of death. Have you ever noticed how many people die near their birthdays? Actress and comedian Betty White passed on December 31, 2021, and she would have turned 100-year-old on January 17, 2022.

Prophet Nostradamus predicted the exact day of his death on July 2, 1566, dying of natural causes.

Morpheus: *Have you ever had a dream, Neo, that you seemed so sure it was real? But if you were unable to wake up from that dream, how would you tell the difference between the dream world and the real world?*

Morpheus: *As long as the matrix exists, the human race will never be free. —The Matrix* movie 1999

CHAPTER 15

THE MATRIX

What is reality? Is our world real or is it a dream within a dream? Do we live in a computer simulation? As a small child, I believed humans were controlled by gods (or perhaps aliens) hidden behind the curtain at the controls (a reference to *The Wizard of Oz*). I am not sure how I came up with such an outrageous idea. Perhaps when I had a vision of my sister dying as a child, I believed that by walking backward for a day, she'd reverse her early demise. She listened to me despite thinking I was nuts and survived her childhood, passing at age fifty, which was young.

Recently, the renowned NYU Professor David Chalmers put forward an intriguing response to the argument stemming from the hypothesis that we live in a computer simulation. He argues that even if you did live in a computer simulation, you would still know many of the ordinary things that you think you know. The reason he gives is that if you lived in a computer simulation, though your thoughts and words would have the same meanings as they currently have, they would be about virtual objects and properties, and your thoughts about those objects and properties would be true.

For instance, if you were a virtual being living in a computer simulation, though your concept of ' body' would have the same meaning it currently has, it would be about virtual bodies. Since you would have a virtual body if you lived in a computer simulation, your belief that you have a body would be true. By the same token, your thoughts about trees and birds would be about virtual trees and virtual birds.

It gets really confusing, but there is a point to these theories.

Imagine that you take a red pill like Neo did in the movie *The Matrix*, and discovered that you have been living in a computer simulation all along. Like Neo, you would be traumatized, and resent your prior deception. This calls into question Chalmers' claim that if we lived in a computer simulation, many of our terms, such as 'tree', 'body', and so forth would mean what they currently do, but be about virtual objects and processes. And it calls into question the claim that even if we did live in a computer simulation, we would nevertheless know many of the things we think we know.

One popular move is to reject the skeptic's assumption that the only thing you may rely on to rule out the possibility that you live in a computer simulation is your sensory experience. Normally, we think of our reasons for belief as involving not just our sensory experiences, but the facts that those experiences are about, or more broadly, the facts that we know.

Nevertheless, since we cannot tell whether we live in a computer simulation, you cannot know whether you know that you have a body and that everything in our physical world really exists. This may leave you with an eerie feeling.

Then who is the programmer of our world? God? Aliens or artificial intelligence?

In 2001, Nick Bostrom, a philosopher at the University of Oxford, distributed a draft of a paper suggesting that a highly advanced supercomputer—with a mass on the order of a planet, would be capable of running a simulation on a humanity-sized scale. In an interview with Vulture Magazine, Bostrom claimed he hadn't seen *The Matrix* before publishing the paper.

Bostrom said this computer would be capable of doing 10^{42} calculations per second, and it could simulate the entire history of humankind (including all our thoughts, feelings, and memories) by using less than one-millionth of its processing power for just one second.

From his logic, he concluded that all of humanity and our entire physical universe are just blips of data stored in the hard drive of a massive supercomputer. He stated, "We are almost certainly characters living in a computer simulation." Almost 15 years later, Elon Musk reiterated Bostrum's ideas. Musk said at the 2016 Recode Conference that he thinks "the odds that we're in base reality is one in billions." Bostrum is still thinking and talking about the fraught relationship between humans and computers. In a speech at a TED conference, he put forward the frightening idea that humanity could destroy itself with a technology of our own creation. Bostrom went on to suggest that the way to save us from ourselves is simple—by mass surveillance using AI.

There's also the theory that we live in a holographic universe. Stephen Hawking played with the idea that our universe, with its beginning in the Big Bang, is one of an infinite number of coexisting bubble universes. There are many different theories about the bubble universe. It and many interacting worlds theories are slight deviations from the multiverse theory.

Some distant two-dimensional surface contains all the data needed to describe our world, similar to a hologram, the data is projected to appear in three dimensions. Like the characters on a TV screen, we live on a flat surface that happens to look like it has depth.

This sounds crazy, but for physicists, the laws of physics make more sense when written in two dimensions than three. This is Quantum thinking that we are co-creators with God, and in mass thinking, we are creating our chaotic world through our fears, hate, distrust, anger, and disunity. Quantum theory is modern physics that explains the nature and behavior of matter and energy on the atomic and subatomic levels. It all comes down to energy and frequency.

Is the supercomputer in the Cosmos, God's mind? Are we merely illusions of God believing that we are real? Remember we are all made up of molecules and atoms, in constant motion, although we can't see them. What holds atoms together? Chemical bonds and electrons or something we can't even imagine.

Another intriguing hypothesis is about the reverse universe. While a group of NASA scientists worked on an experiment in Antarctica, they detected evidence of a parallel universe. The experts used a giant balloon to carry NASA's Antarctic Impulsive Transient Antenna, or ANITA, high above Antarctica, where the frigid, dry air provided the perfect environment with little to no radio noise to distort its findings. It detected high-energy particles can only becoming "down" from space, going back up into space.

They are called neutrinos. The discovery implies that these particles are traveling backward in time, suggesting evidence of a parallel universe. Principal ANITA investigator Peter Gorham, an experimental particle physicist at the University of Hawaii, suggested that the only way the tau neutrino could behave that way is if it changed into a different type of particle before passing through the Earth and then back again. Gorham, the lead author of a Cornell University paper described the odd phenomenon, noting that he and his fellow researchers had seen several of these "impossible events," which some were skeptical about. Not everyone was comfortable with the hypothesis. NASA was one of the first agencies to try and quell public excitement about the find and so they went to great pains to silence and discredit the scientists.

Perhaps the simplest explanation for this anomaly is that at the moment of the Big Bang 13.5 billion years ago, two universes were formed—our world and another parallel world that is running in reverse with time going backward. If any inhabitants of this universe existed, they'd probably consider us the backward ones. It would in essence be a Benjamin Button universe where you'd never age.

There's every indication that we are experiencing a reverse world now where everything is backward. Our lives turned upside down with COVID-19 in 2020, there's no justice even with the Supreme Justices, our borders are no longer safe, crime is out of control, the media give us false news, and the Earth is in a cataclysmic cycle. Politicians that we once trusted can no longer be trusted. The paranormal is becoming the normal as other worlds merge into our world. People are seeing bizarre objects and UFOs in the night sky, and nature is behaving in ways we've never seen before. It appears we are in a "reverse world."

Multiverses

A multiverse is a hypothetical group of multiple universes, and together these universes comprise of everything that exists; space, time, matter, energy, information, and physical laws. The idea that there is more than just one universe like ours in the cosmos, seems silly. There have to be separate universes.

Scientists have always applied the theories to our universe, but what if the laws of physics in this universe don't apply in other universes?

What if we are a computer simulation in God's mind, and that anything is possible? And here's another thought—what if what is currently taking place on our planet from the anger, fear, sadness, violence, and hate has been created by us and our chaotic thoughts. In other words, we are the programmers of our world. If we stopped buying into the constant fear, our world would instantly change for the better. Humans are addicted to fear. How many of you watch television dramas and thrive on them? Our human programmers also use television to control us—what we buy, eat and believe.

I have always known there are parallel worlds that sometimes slip into our world, and there are multiverses out there. There are time slips and time travelers who insert new programs into the universe, changing our world from time to time. We live in one big computer.

Our world is one of a free-will world, and anything goes here. That's why they continue to control us like sheep by those who think they own us—from the government to beings that reside on Earth or visit Earth from other realms.

The system we live in has become corrupted and anyone who doesn't honor life or the planet, will fall big time. Consciousness must change for us to evolve and realize that what we've been told about our compartmentalized lives is a lie. Open the door and view an incredible world of magic and things that would blow your mind.

Holographic 3-D technology is being used by the movie industry, but there are those advanced beings who have used holographic inserts to control us through the ages. They create dramas that look real that aren't and insert them in portals or stargates to hoodwink humanity. It's been quite effective. They change information to one of disinformation. Many of the UFOs in the sky are holographic inserts that appear real and can even show up on radar. That's how advanced they have become with sciences and technology.

Our religious beliefs have been created by these inserts. They've been used to move humanity to the one world order of control. They don't want you informed, they want to keep ancient wisdom from you and the truth of your reality. They are hoping you stay comatose in your comfy world of material things, and never realize that one day you have no freedom—none whatsoever!

Welcome to 2022, where everyone is controlled.

They have also used Prime Events to control us. A Prime Event can be for the good of humanity or another ploy to control us. For instance, the Harmonic Convergence on August 16-17, 1987, was organized by Dr. Jose Argüelles without the aid of the internet. This was the world's first synchronized global peace meditation. The event coincided with an exceptional alignment of the planets in the Solar System.

Many of you may have a feeling of déjà vu and you have experienced this all before. You have! You are experiencing your multidimensional memory of the times you have gone to other systems and done the same thing. Most of us lost our memories because we became humans. You knew before you arrived that losing your memory was part of the process of reincarnation.

Prime events, in the negative, are created to alter the timelines such as President John F. Kennedy's assassination on November 22, 1963, and the events of September 11, 2001, that created horror, anger, and profound grief around the world. Think how our world changed suddenly on those specific dates. With 9-11 more of our freedom vanished and freedom continues to vanish. The COVID-19 pandemic is another primary event that has been used to bring about tyranny against humanity.

In Barbara Marciniak's book, *Earth—Pleiadian Keys to the Living Library,* she writes that our future is being penetrated from the outside—from the future. Some have incredible knowledge about probabilities and how to insert themselves into the variable of electromagnetic portals. If the corridors are not traveled with knowledge, many events can blindly trample through what is called time, moving from one place to another like tidal waves pulverizing existence.

To establish a new timeline and a whole new web, the event that anchors time, must be a profound implosion that affects all of existence. Otherwise, the web has nowhere to go. Those who own the timeline to Earth have been keeping Earth segregated, and not allowing free commerce to come and go on the timeline.

Timelines, the fabric of time, and the tubes that run on this fabric of time are all hooked into primary events. Without a primary event, you cannot hook into a timeline. In other words, the secondary and tertiary webs need to be hooked into a primary event, so that other timelines can use it as an anchor. The splitting of the atom was another primary event.

A primary event can be considered an event that is a turning point for the domain in which it transpires. As mentioned earlier, the Harmonic Convergence was a primary event that changed the course of history drastically. It was an orchestrated event impulse from the future. It was sent from the future into the past and then reorganized into the present to create a hole through which the secondary and tertiary nets could be built and find a link to the planet. If these webs needed a primary event to link onto, what was the primary event that gave them power and the hold? Simply put, it was the consciousness of masses of humans coming together in prayer and intent to reform the future.

Unfortunately, this knowledge is in the hands of the Family of Dark, and they have misused it to control Earth and humans for eons. Some own the corridors of time or believe they do. They are reconstructing the prime corridors and organizing new eras of existence. Once these corridors are built, many forms of intelligence will be able to move back and forth, with the so-called owners of these corridors determining which forces are allowed to enter. Right now those of lower vibrations and darker entities entering our world like never before. Do you think it's a coincidence that huge numbers of humans are hooked on drugs that allow lower entities to enter their bodies and enter our world? They are the possessed.

The current problem on Earth is why there has been a great influx of life forms that have been using the human species for experimentation. When the last stretch of time is completed, there will be a dimensional shift upon this planet.

We are already entering a parallel universe. We can change the past as well as the future by learning to play the game.

Humans must learn to control frequencies. Some are compatible and others are incompatible with humans. The more we grow in consciousness and maintain the frequency of love, the more we will be able to alter the incompatible frequencies into benign energies. Sometimes the greatest enlightenment comes from a catastrophic event. State of mind is the name of the game in our reality. We are a dream in God's mind, believing that what we see, hear and feel is real when nothing is real. It's called *Maya*, the grand illusion! In the Advaita Vedanta school of Hindu philosophy, Maya, "appearance", is "the powerful force that creates the cosmic illusion that the phenomenal world is real." Maya exists so Self could experience Love.

I suspect that even the energy we call God is learning about itself, growing, and evolving. Nothing stays stagnant in the universe of time and space. Everything changes and everything is evolving toward the Light.

CHAPTER 16

THE POWER OF AUM OR OM

Everything in our world is frequency and in the entire Universe. Can you imagine if humans throughout the world began chanting to raise dark lower vibrational forces encompassing the world now? I can! A superwave of untold magnitude would transform our world instantly.

The first impulse to emerge from the silence of the absolute, or the field of Pure Potentiality, was the sound "OM" or more correctly "AUM," according to the *Vedas* (ancient Hindu scriptures). Even the Bible and modern science agree that the initial spark of creation came from sound or vibration. The Gospel, according to John says, "In the beginning was the Word and the Word was with God and the Word was God ... and the Word was made flesh."

If you substitute "Word" with "Sound," it becomes, "In the beginning was the Sound and the Sound was God ... and the Sound became manifest."

In modern science, they talk about the Big Bang Theory, again sound.

It's this original, primordial sound that diversified: "The One became many." Each separate vibration evolved to reflect the whole in infinite disguises, giving rise to the world in which we live. Universes within universes, each vibrating at their own frequency, interacted with every other frequency to produce a variety of life. Every organ, tissue, and cell has its vibration which, when in harmony, creates the most wonderful symphony imaginable, the human body.

If disharmony arises or a break in the unfolding of the vibration occurs, there develops a loss of wholeness leading to discomfort and disease.

Sound has been used since the beginning of history to create certain moods in the listener. Different sounds affect people in different ways. Fingernails scraping a blackboard elicit a very different reaction than a violin (unless it's being played by a 6-year-old). Shamanic drumming can create a trance-like state, marching bands are used to fire-up an army or sports team, and a mother's lullaby soothes a troubled child. The different ragas of Indian classical music are attuned to different times of the day or different seasons to harmonize the listener with the rhythms of nature.

With the right sounds, you can align yourself with the vibrations that foster health, happiness, and unity. Vibrational music can enhance the growth of plants, toning can alter your vibrational rate and produce healing. It's the process of allowing sound to move through you as if you were playing an instrument. Plants feel you when you walk through a garden and touch a plant. It's communicating with other plants. Scientists have now learned that plants and trees communicate with each other. When we dedicate toning to animals, plants, and Earth, we are connected to everything and that energizes and realigns our connection to Mother Earth.

If you listen to Tibetan toning/chanting, you will hear different tones, opening portals in our world. When you visit an energy vortex or leyline area and intend to release energy that has been stored there, you can tone to merge yourself with that power site. Ancient stone structures contain information stored within them like a recording.

Learn what is a good frequency is compared to one that controls you like television and video games. This control is used to transmit fear quickly to the masses. Those of you who ween yourself from television will live healthier and longer lives. If you must have a television set, unplug it from your home. Frequency waves are transmitted through the airwaves even when it is shut off and plugged in.

Drumming, singing bowls, and chanting raise your vibrational rate. Consider if a large number of humans did this in unison what could happen—there would be an instant transmutation of Earth's energy. It would be a shockwave! Listen to nature's broadcast inside and learn from the Living Library of Earth.

Parthenis was told by the oracle, during a visit to Delphi with her husband Mnesarchus, that she would bear a son who would outshine all men in beauty and wisdom, and who would be a benefactor to mankind. The child prodigy, Pythagoras, was born sometime between 600 and 590 B.C. at Sidon in Phoenicia, although his parents' hometown was Samos. After his birth, Parthenis changed her name to Pythasis in honor of the Pythian priestess who made the prophecy.

Many believed Pythagoras was a god in mortal form. And his birth was like Jesus—both were believed to be divinely conceived (the God Apollo was rumored to be Pythagoras' father), both were born in Syria, both births were prophesied and both men were born when their parents were journeying away from home. Because of these similarities, Pythagoras was often known as "the son of God" and was believed to be under the influence of divine guidance.

Pythagoras traveled widely during his early years and visited many countries including Greece, Egypt, Phoenicia, Syria, Babylon, Media, Persia, and Hindustan. Jesus was rumored to have traveled to many countries and given sacred knowledge. During Pythagoras's travels, he acquired great knowledge and wisdom; he was initiated into Eleusinian Mysteries, the Mysteries of Isis at Thebes, the mysteries of Adonis, and the secret teachings of the Chaldeans. He was the first man to use the word "philosopher" whenever he described himself— previously wise men were known as sages.

Pythagoras finally settled at Crotona in Southern Italy in 525 BC where he founded a religious/philosophical society, better known as the Italic or Pythagorean School, to pass on his arcane wisdom to a select group of followers. He married one of his pupils during his early sixties. The marriage produced seven children.

He was described as an impressive-looking man, over six feet tall with a perfect body like that of the god Apollo. He grew strong and more powerful with age and was considered to be in the prime of his life at the time of his assassination at age 100 if the story is true. Like most geniuses, Pythagoras was very outspoken and created many enemies. Another story claims that one of his enemies instigated a mob against the Pythagoreans and set fire to the building where they were staying. However, Pythagoras was able to escape. He then went to Metapontum and starved himself to death around the year 495 B.C.

Luckily the doctrines of Pythagoras were always closely guarded by his followers and after his death, they managed to preserve a great deal of his work. His work and teachings greatly influenced the Greek philosopher Plato (c. 429-326 BC).

Pythagoras, like the philosophers of the Ionian school, wanted to determine what the basic cosmic substance was, and also attempted a scientific explanation of the universe in terms of Ionian naturalism (Thales believed that all substances were variants of water and Heraclitus believed that they were variants of fire). However, Pythagoras took a more Orphic approach and believed his first principle of the universe was *number.*

The Pythagoreans had a proverb that stated, "all things are assimilated to number" and were taught that number determined the harmonies of music and of the spheres, the movements of the sun, moon, and stars, and the proportions of architecture. However, Pythagoras believed that the world was built on the power of number and that it was easy to identify number with everything good, beautiful, orderly, right, and proper. In his *Sacred Discourse* he states that "number is the ruler of forms and ideas and the cause of gods and demons."

Members of his society were expected to observe secrecy and strict loyalty to their order like the belief in the transmigration of souls, a basis for their way of life. Pythagoras was able to remember previous incarnations and for this reason, was thought to know more than others. He was never addressed as Pythagoras, but instead by *The Master* or *That Man*. This might have been because his name was believed to consist of a certain number of specially arranged letters that had great sacred significance or because students were initiated using a secret formula concealed within the letters of his name.

His followers were bound by very strict rules of conduct for the religious life—they wore white clothing and were required to observe sexual purity. They thought that if their souls were purified with music and mental activity they could reach higher incarnations. The god of Pythagoras was the Monad—the One that is Everything. He described God as the Supreme Mind, the Cause, Intelligence, and Power within all things. He saw the motion of God as circular with a body made of light and a nature composed of truth. The students were trained in gymnastics and the study of geometry, music, and astronomy, all essential to a rational understanding of God, man, or nature. Pythagoras taught moderation in all things, and although he and his students did not totally abstain from eating meat, they followed an essentially vegetarian diet.

Pythagoras is usually credited with the discovery of the relationship between sound and numbers. There is a story that after Pythagoras passed a forge he noticed that the four different sized anvils produced different notes when struck with a hammer. Upon further investigation, he found that their weights were in the proportions 6,8, 9, and 12. When he later suspended four weights of the same proportions on strings he discovered, to his satisfaction, that when he plucked the strings he could reproduce the same four notes that he obtained from the anvils. When the lengths of the strings were doubled the new notes produced were an octave above the original notes. Therefore the octave could be expressed numerically as a ratio of 2:1. The other intervals were ratios of 3:2 and 4:3—once again only the first four numbers are required to express these facts.

Pythagoras envisioned the universe as a harmonious whole and believed that everything in it emitted a sound or a "vibration." He viewed the Earth and the planets as globes orbiting around a central luminary. Following his discovery that strings of different lengths produced different notes when plucked, he believed each planet had a note of its own which depended upon its distance from the center. When combined these planetary sounds should produce a "harmonious cosmic octave" more commonly known as the "music of the spheres."

He believed that if sounds could be expressed in terms of

numbers this would provide the key to the mysteries of the universe. The vibration or "tone" of the universe at the exact moment of an individual's birth was believed to influence both his character and his destiny in life.

For those of you who want a more earthly musical composition on the sound of the spheres refer to music composer Gustav Holst (1879-1934) who was introduced to astrology in 1910 and produced the haunting suite *The Planets* corresponding to each astrological sign.

Numbers are represented everywhere in our physical world. The essence and flow of energy of numbers fill the Universe, a cosmic equation that creates our physical and spiritual realms. Everything in the Universe holds a mathematical signature, emitting a musical tone. Together numbers make up a symphony that vibrates through the cosmos, giving each number and note a beautiful and unique spiritual frequency and meaning.

Numerologists believe that we are born on a certain date, hour, and minute not by chance, but to learn important spiritual lessons and to perform specific tasks during our lifetime. Conditions and vibrations prevailing at that precise moment must be favorable if we are to fulfill our mission in life. Reincarnation also plays an important role in their philosophy of life.

It was Honoré de Balzac (1799-1850) the French realistic novelist who, during a conversation on the subject of numbers, said, "Without them, the whole edifice of our civilization would fall to pieces.' Numbers rule everything around us—the cosmos, the Universe, the Earth the planets, and the stars."

Numbers are called the physical constants of the universe, and without them, you wouldn't exist. These mysterious numbers describe things like the speed of light or the strength of the electromagnetic force that holds atoms and molecules together. Our fundamental theories of how the universe works rely on these numbers, but scientists have no idea where they come from. There are two types of physical constant—ones where the numerical value depends on the units you use and others where it is always the same.

The Old Testament Book of Genesis describes how the Universe was created by the "Word of God" which was probably a vibration, a sound that had enormous force and creation. The ancients believed that sound at certain frequencies could be used for creation or destruction. Today we know it's a scientific fact that certain frequencies can kill; even a soprano's high note can shatter a glass. The ancients also believed that it was possible to discover and apply the "word of God" for their own needs. Special words and music were used for invocations and the success achieved was thought to depend on the vibration and the pitch of the sound chosen because music, as well as words, can be related to numbers. It is believed the low vibrations are destructive and the higher vibrations are healing.

Vibration played a destructive role in the collapse of the 1940 Tacoma Narrows Bridge, a suspension bridge in the State of Washington that spanned the Tacoma Narrows strait of Puget Sound between Tacoma and the Kitsap Peninsula. It opened to traffic on July 1, 1940, and collapsed into the Puget Sound on November 7 of the same year (strange it happened on the 7th day). The date seemed to be connected to the event.

At the time of its construction and destruction, the bridge was the third-longest suspension bridge in the world in terms of main span length, behind the Golden Gate Bridge and the George Washington Bridge. From the time the deck was built, it began to move vertically in windy conditions, which lead to construction workers dubbing it "Galloping Gertie." The motion was detected during the time it opened to the public, and several measures to stop it proved to be ineffective.

The bridge finally collapsed under a 40-mile-per hour (64km/h) wind conditions on the morning of November 7, 1940.

The bridge's collapse changed science and engineering in many ways. In physics textbooks, the event is presented as an example of elementary forced resonance, with the wind providing an external periodic frequency that matched the bridge's natural structural frequency. However, many believed the failure was due to aeroelastic flutter. The bridge's failure increased the research in the field of bridge aerodynamics-aeroelastics, the study of which has influenced the designs of all the world's great long-span bridges built since 1940.

The number 7 was significant in the destruction of the walls of Jericho. According to the Book of Joshua, the Battle of Jericho was the first battle of the Israelites in their conquest of Canaan. According to Joshua 6:1-27, the walls of Jericho fell after Joshua's Israelite army marched around the city blowing their trumpets.

"Now Jericho was shut up inside and outside because of the people of Israel. None went out, and none came in. And the Lord said to Joshua, "See, I have given Jericho into your hand, with its king and mighty men of valor. You shall march around the city, all the men of war going around the city once. Thus shall you do for six days. Seven priests shall bear seven trumpets of rams' horns before the ark. On the seventh day, you shall march around the city seven times, and the priests shall blow the trumpets. And when they make a long blast with the ram's horn, when you hear the sound of the trumpet, then all the people shall shout with a great shout, and the wall of the city will fall down flat, and the people shall go up, everyone straight before him." ...

So, is it possible mechanical resonance from marching around the city of Jericho caused the collapse of the walls? Acoustical resonance can produce the collapse of bridges and buildings as demonstrated by earthquakes and winds. Who knows what happened during Joshua's time, but we do know that sound is powerful stuff. We might also ask how Joshua obtained such an advanced weapon. Or was it pure luck that he instructed his people to march and sound their horns resulting in mechanical and acoustical resonance? I'd say he knew the properties of resonance through the Ark of the Covenant. Then Joshua said to the people, *"Consecrate yourselves, for tomorrow the LORD will do wonders among you."*

And Joshua spoke to the priests, saying, "Take up the ark of the covenant and cross over ahead of the people." So they took up the ark of the covenant and went ahead of the people.

Now the LORD said to Joshua, *"This day I will begin to exalt you in the sight of all Israel, that they may know that just as I have been with Moses, I will be with you...."*

On July 5, 2011, a 39-story office/shopping center building in Seoul, South Korea started to shake rapidly. For ten minutes vertical tremors violently rocked the building, causing an immediate evacuation of the premises. After the shaking subsided, engineers began a lengthy process to determine the cause of the incident. Eliminating earthquakes and windstorms, the culprit appeared to be an aerobics class of 23 people on a mid-level floor. Their Tae Bo workout was twice as intense that day, making their footwork synch up with the building's structural resonance.

More recently, London's Millennium Bridge was shut down in 2000 after a crowd created oscillating waves across the deck of the bridge. Like pushing a child on a swing at the correct moment so that her motion is amplified, resonance's effects are caused by the well-timed push of each individual wave. Push the swing at the right moment, and you could send the kid flying; amplify the vibrations in a building's structure enough, and you can cause it to collapse.

Infrasound and Humans

Resonance in audio waves and glassware is probably the most classic example of waves affecting the structure. An example of that is the large lady shattering a wine glass with her pitch-perfect operatic voice. But most people don't know about infrasound. Such sound waves, lower in frequency than 20 Hz, lower than human hearing, can be used for monitoring earthquakes, charting rock and petroleum formations below the Earth, and also in ballistocardiography and seimocardiography. Humans can still detect them subconsciously and resonate against the body with terrifying results.

In 2003, a team of UK scientists experimented with the emotional effects of infrasonic resonance by exposing a group of 700 people to two identical musical pieces, except one was laced with inaudible 17 Hz sound waves. The audience's response to the laced concert was obvious—anxiety, uneasiness, extreme sorrow, nervous feelings of revulsion or fear, chills down the spine, and feelings of pressure on the chest. The emotional disturbance of infrasonic waves is so strong that they are considered the best theory for ghost sightings.

Predictably, these waves that cause awe and fear in humans, have already been weaponized. Military engineers have created acoustic bazookas that generate infrasonic waves in a directed form. A ten-second exposure to such waves that travel through concrete walls, will lead to severe, crippling nausea. Although no one is admitting it is in use, it is believed this weapon was used at the American and Canadian Embassy in Havana, Cuba in 2016, referred to as the "Havana Syndrome." The symptoms range in severity from pain and ringing in the ears to cognitive difficulties.

In 2017, U.S. intelligence and military personnel and their families reported the same symptoms in China, Europe, and Washington, D.C.

Can you imagine if this technology was used on millions of people? It is, and it's going to get worse. They can control our moods, our emotions, our illness in infrasound!

Nikola Tesla – Master of Resonance

Nikola Tesla (1856-1943) once stated he could split the Earth in half through vibration or resonance, and his experiments may have proven he had that technology. He has been called "A Man out of Time" because of his futuristic experiments, inventions, and patents.

He discovered the power of resonance with an innocent experiment in 1898. Tesla attached a small vibrator to an iron column in his New York City laboratory and started it vibrating. At certain frequencies, specific pieces of equipment in the room began to jiggle. Change the frequency and the jiggle moved to another part of the room. Unfortunately, he hadn't accounted for the fact that the column ran downward into the foundation beneath the building. His vibrations were being transmitted all over Manhattan.

For Tesla, the first hint of trouble came when the walls and floors heave. He stopped the experiment just as the police crashed through his door. He had caused neighborhood windows to break, buildings to sway, and people to rush into the streets panicked. This was Tesla's oscillator which became known as a reciprocating electricity generator.

Although Tesla was not the first to discover resonance, he was obsessed with it and created some of the most incredible demonstrations of it. Pythagoras experimented with it, and most likely there were others before Pythagoras. Tesla studied both mechanical and electrical versions. In the process, he was the first to create an artificial earthquake, numerous artificial lightning storms, could knock an entire power plant off-line in Colorado, and nearly caused the steel frame of a skyscraper under construction in Manhattan to collapse. He realized that the principles of resonance could be used to transmit and receive radio messages well before Marconi. In fact, knowledgeable sources now credit Tesla as the inventor of the radio rather than Marconi. This includes what the Supreme Court ruled in 1943 that Tesla's radio patents had proceeded all others including Marconi's patents.

Tesla's obsession with pursuing grand ideas and projects proved to be his undoing. He became convinced that energy could be transmitted through the air without wires and spent a small future on a demonstration project. He built a giant Tesla coil in Colorado which used electrical resonance to build up incredible high voltages and caused fantastic lightning displays. Unfortunately, his dream of transmitting wireless power was never commercialized due to his decline in health and money. He died in New York City at age 87.

Conspiracy theorists believe that his papers mysteriously vanished after his death were taken by the U.S. military and used in the HAARP experiments in Alaska. HAARP (High-Frequency Active Auroral Research Program) is a little-known, yet critically important U.S. military defense program which has generated quite a bit of controversy and conspiracy over the years in certain circles. Though denied by HAARP officials, some respected researchers allege that the secret electromagnetic warfare capabilities of HAARP are designed to forward the US military's stated goal of achieving full-spectrum dominance by the year 2020. Others go so far as to claim that HAARP can and has been used for weather modification creating earthquakes and tsunamis, disrupting global communications systems, and more.

Everything in our world vibrates—we know that because everything is made up of atoms and molecules that vibrate.

The vibration of atomic particles, including electrons and nuclei, is a quantum phenomenon. There are discreet energy levels of vibration with no "in-between." Recent research has also found that the atoms on the surface of a solid object vibrate at specific rates (frequencies), but not at rates in between.

The vibratory rate of the human body has been determined to be between 62 and 68 MHz (megahertz). The human brain functions optimally between 72 and 90 MHz. When the body vibration lowers to 58 MHz, we can catch a cold; at 57 MHZ, we get the flu; at 55 MHz candida, 52 MHz Epstein Barr; 42 MHZ cancer sets in, and at 25 MHz death begins.

I believe that some want to eliminate us by lowering vibrations through bad food, fast food, pharmaceutical drugs, recreational drugs, abuse of alcohol, canned foods, and maybe even chemtrails that continue to cover our skies. Radiation from TV and computer screens also lowers the MHz of the body. The vibrational rate of Earth, humans, and Earth's creatures has reached a critical point. We can turn the low vibrations into high vibrations by awaking and honoring Earth and our own bodies. I'll admit the picture at this very moment is beyond discouraging. However, there are many scenarios to be played out in our holographic world and all is not hopeless. It is up to us, "the ground crew," to ensure our world continues on and we survive.

The number 7 has great power and has been mythologized for centuries. Christianity and Islam grew out of ancient Mesopotamia, and some of the region's most ancient archaeological evidence revealed that the number 7 had cosmic significance. Their creation story is alluded to as the *Seven Tablets of Creation*.

Seven has always been a very special number. Sanskrit's most ancient holy book, the *Rig Vega*, describes seven stars, seven concentric continents, and seven streams of soma, the drink of the gods. According to the Jewish and Christian Old Testament, the world was created in seven days and Noah's dove returned seven days after the Flood.

Similarly, the Egyptians mapped seven paths to heaven, Allah created the seven-layered Islamic heaven and earth, and the newborn Buddha took seven strides. For numerologists, seven signifies creation, because it is the sum of the spiritual three and the material four; for alchemists, there are clear parallels between the seven steps leading up to King Solomon's temple and the seven successive stages of chemical and spiritual purification. Iranian cats have seven lives, seven deities bring good luck in Japan, and a traditional Jewish cure for fever entailed taking seven prickles from seven palm trees and seven nails from seven doors."

From Science: A Four Thousand Year History by Patricia Fara (2009) in her Freemasonry book wrote: "This mystical ladder, which in Masonry is referred to 'the theological ladder, which Jacob in his vision saw, reached from Earth to heaven,' was widely dispersed among the religions of antiquity, where it was always supposed to consist of 7 rounds or steps. For instance, in the Mysteries of Mithras, in Persia, where there were 7 stages or degrees of initiation, they were erected in temples, or rather caves, for it was in them that the initiation was conducted. It was a high ladder, of seven steps or gates.

In the *Mysteries of Brahma*, we find the same reference to the ladder of seven steps; but here the names were different.

Seven steps were emblematical of the 7 worlds which constituted the Indian universe. The lowest was the Earth; the second, the World of Reexistence; the third, Heaven; the fourth, the Middle World, or intermediate region between the lower and upper worlds; the fifth, the World of Births, in which souls are again born; the sixth, the Mansion of the Blessed; and the seventh, or topmost round, the Sphere of Truth, the abode of Brahma, he himself being but a symbol of the sun."

In *The Symbolism of Freemasonry* by Albert G. Mackey (1869) Greek Pythagoreans believed that the number 7 pointed symbolically to the union of the Deity with the universe. This association was picked up by the Christian church, especially during the Middle Ages. Seven was regarded as having sacred power, such as in the 7 cardinal virtues, the 7 deadly sins, the 7 sacraments, etc. Thus, it was assumed that there must be exactly 7 planets.

The number 7 is used 735 times in the Bible, and in numerology seven refers to wisdom, divine protection, and power.

CHAPTER 17

CHEMTRAILS

In 2014, an Airforce pilot told a friend's friend that he was fired because he knew about the global engineering of chemtrails, known as "Indigo Sky Fold." He said the pilots are told to fly certain routes in the sky, and they are rotated constantly so they never stay long in one place to make friends and talk about their missions. He didn't agree with his mission assignments but as he said, "what officer truly does? Several of us have thought of bucking the ranks and going AWOL from time to time. We are kept in the dark about what we are really spraying. If they should get wind that we or any of our family members are inquiring actively active and swift disciplinary will be taken. I would not intentionally spray my family and children with aerosols"

Extreme weather, record-breaking heat in the summer of 2020, have created unimaginable wildfires that have destroyed hundreds of homes, and some lives in California, Oregon,

Washington, and Idaho. At the beginning of the year, I had a vision of wildfires raging through thousands of acres, consuming everything in their path, and how drought conditions made it easy for arsonists to start the fires. However, not all the fires were started by arsonists. Some started from lightning or careless campers.

What caused the pine trees and all the brush to become so flammable in the past twenty years? What caused the pine trees to be unable to fight against the beetle invasions when they had survived the insects for centuries?

I, among other conspiracy theorists, believe the chemtrails that began in the late 1990s, have contributed to global warming as well as fossil fuels and caused a massive die-off of trees and other plants.

Strange still was the way Coronavirus swept across the globe in record time and killed nearly one million souls at the time. I was shown the horrible flu late in 2019 that would be like the Spanish Flu, but at the time I couldn't conceive of such a horrible pandemic because of our advanced medical technology since the flu of 1917. Little did I foresee how it would affect our lives so drastically, and how thousands of humans would be infected throughout the world. Coronavirus was different from any flu humans had ever had due to China's biological experiments and carelessness.

Unfortunately, humans haven't learned that technology in the wrong hands can be our ultimate extinction.

You see, I grew up when my generation, the Baby Boomers, believed that we would see the Age of Aquarius where love and peace abounded in our world. But it was only a dream and not reality.

Earth is experiencing increased seismic and volcanic activity while our Sun stays strangely quiet—few sunspots. Birds continue to fall from the sky dead, and sea creatures and insects, and bees are dying *en masse* all over the world.

During this year, I have received countless email questions that I couldn't answer each email personally. I will include those questions in this book and answer them from what I have seen in visions and sense intuitively will happen in 2022. If we thought 2020, was crazy, you haven't seen anything yet. 2022 will bring about massive changes to humanity in so many ways both positive and negative—but it will be a tumultuous year in politics, earth changes, weather anomalies, UFOs, medicine, travel, and saber-rattling countries.

Beginning in the late 1990s, I photographed and studied the chemtrail phenomenon and noted how the chemtrails always became heavy with crisscrossed patterns in the sky before an approaching weather front. Whenever rain was forecast, clouds formed but there was no precipitation. It was odd. Then others began investigating the chemtrails spread by white, unmarked jets, and the conspiracy spread worldwide that a huge covert operation was in place.

In the past five years, we have witnessed unimaginable wildfires in the western United States and the rainforests of Brazil.

Author Denis Mills discovered an alarming link between chemtrails and the super wildfires while researching his novel, *Matt Legend—Veil of Lies*. He discovered that unprecedented levels of aluminum and barium nano-dust, primary components in chemtrails, both of which are incendiary, are fueling the ferocity of the super wildfires.

A retired USAF brigadier general, Gen. Charles Jones, has been quoted from a public source as stating, "These white aircraft spraying trails are the result of scientifically verifiable spraying of aluminum particles and other toxic heavy metals, polymers and chemicals. Millions of tons of aluminum and barium are being sprayed almost daily across the U.S., stated Mills, a former naval officer, and UCLA graduate. "Just sprinkle aluminum or barium dust on fire and see what happens. It's near explosive. When wildfires break out, the aluminum/barium dust results in levels of fire intensity so great as to cause firefighters to coin a new term— 'firenadoes,' " he said.

The government has denied the existence of chemtrail spraying for years. However, it is now called by various names under geoengineering.

According to Cal Fire Operation Chief Steve Crawford, the fires are burning differently and more aggressively. It has been reported the fires move faster than anyone has ever seen before and the barriers that in years past contained them, such as rivers, no longer work.

Another interesting fact—in Northern California's Mt. Shasta region, Francis Mangel, a USDA biologist took samples of water and soil and found elevated levels of aluminum in them—4,610 parts per million which are 25,000 times the safe guidelines of the WHO (World Health Organization). The entire U.S., in addition to various other NATO countries, has been sprayed.

On March 23, 2018, the Richmond County Daily Journal in Rockingham, North Carolina ran this article by Robert Lee who calls himself a concerned citizen and a U.S. Marine veteran who owns and operates Rockingham Guns and Ammo. I can relate to everything he wrote in this article and what I have witnessed since childhood.

"I'm not a conspiracy theorist, not at all. All I have to say is, it's time that I write about a subject that was brought to my attention eight years ago. When the subject of chemtrails came up, I just shrugged it off and let it go. I did not think much about it. I, of course, did from time to time see these long trails coming out of aircraft that were at a great height. They were at an altitude that was greater than any commercial aircraft I had seen flying over. Still, at the time it did not matter to me. Today it's a different story. Something is taking place and I do not believe it's a good thing.

"To start I need to go back a bit. Remember when, as children, we saw the first jet aircraft going over? It was unbelievable, to say the least. It was a great sight for a child. Then the sonic boom would come from the aircraft breaking the sound barrier. I can still remember the trails of white smoke coming out, or that was what I thought it was. As it turned out, it was water vapor. These vapor trails are contrails, which are the condensation from the aircraft. Those trails lasted for but seconds as the aircraft flew through the sky. Those trails were about 1,000 feet long or so. My point: they did not last that long at all.

"Now today things have changed. When these military aircraft come over, the trails go from horizon to horizon. One February two years ago I finally saw one of the aircraft itself. Until that day, all I had ever seen was the chemtrails and nothing more. As I sat there — and I sat there for several hours — watching what turned out to be very unnatural, I watched as these chemtrails dropped lower. As they dropped, they got wider. It was at that time that these clouds, for that is what they looked like at that point, started doing funny things. Things that normal clouds do not do. They started rolling over and twisting onto themselves. I also did take notice that the entire county had been checker-boarded in this pattern. In time, what began as a blue cloudless morning sky was no more. The whole county had a cloud over it.

"It was on that day that I did start paying more attention to these chemtrails. The government, in the beginning, stated that they had nothing to do with it. But now they have changed their story and have admitted to the spraying. One point to bring out: They say it's nothing to be concerned about. You keep on believing that. I have no trust in our government to ever tell us the truth about anything. I know firsthand just how rotten our government can be and has been in the past. We cannot trust them. To the government, we are nothing but a number to be used and abused. It happens every day and it is taking place right now as I put these words to print. Don't believe one of these written words, go outside on a cloudless day, and find out for yourself. It will be right there for you to see firsthand. Then research it and find out. I am not going to tell you that it takes place every day; still, just look. You will see regular aircraft going over and you can compare the trails.

"I can't tell you what our government is truly doing but I can say I do not believe it is for the benefit of our people. I can tell you what I have found out. Because of the persistence of the conspiracy theory and questions about government involvement, scientists and government agencies around the world have told their citizens that chemtrails are in fact contrails.

"If that were the truth then why the patterns? Our airlines are not the ones that are doing this. It is our military.

"It depends on who you talk to and if they work for the government as to what you are told. So-called experts on atmospheric phenomena within the government will tell you chemtrails do not exist. They will tell you that the contrails are being affected by different things such as wind shear in vertical and horizontal directions. Also, they are affected by temperature, sunlight, and humidity.

"NASA, the EPA, and the FAA have stated that the checkerboard look of the chemtrails is because of the patterns within the flight lanes of the commercial aircraft. The U.S. Air Force stated in a fact sheet that this has been going on from 1953 until the present day. This is another damn lie. I, just like most of you, have been looking at the sky all of my life, and never in the '60s, '70s, or '80s did I see the sky look like this. The Air Force has also stated that from the ground you cannot tell what you are looking at. I have to agree with them on that point, but only if you are totally blind or live in a cave.

Do these people think we are that stupid? The Air Force rebutted chemtrail theories more directly and said that the theories are nothing, but a hoax and they have disproved the existence of chemtrails. They also stated that chemtrails are nothing more than ice crystals. I can see this, maybe, on a winter day but not in July at a height of 500 feet. All this was stated in their fact sheet. The spraying seems to be more constant and the heaviest over the United States and western Europe. In Asia, Japan and Korea are being sprayed. The only country in the area that is not being sprayed at all is China. If you lean toward the conspiracy theory side, then you should not be shocked by the rest of my column. What this spraying is known as is—the genocide spraying operation.

"There have been many independent tests done over the past five years and it does not look good. It has been confirmed that all around our country a cocktail of dangerous and extremely poisonous chemicals is being dispersed. This includes barium, cadmium, nickel, mold spores, yellow fungal mycotoxins, and the best — radioactive thorium. This is not the total list. The one chemical that is being sprayed the most is aluminum. It can cause all sorts of health problems. The chemical primarily attacks the central nervous system and can cause everything from disturbed sleep, nervousness, memory loss, headaches, and emotional instability.

"With that said, have you not noticed how people have changed in recent years? We see every day more and more people dying at a very young age. Look at the mental state of people. Look at all the different drugs that we are using just to maintain our minds. One thing to add is this: Water samples on top of Mount Shasta, California has aluminum levels that are high enough to kill small rodents. The levels are off the chart with the highest being at 4,800 times the maximum contamination level for drinking water. In a recent snow sample, the level was 100 times the level for aluminum in snow.

"Those who work in the field of geoengineering will tell you that the goal is to reduce global warming. Just another lie that we have been told. They got caught. For years, the government denied the idea of chemtrails and geoengineering. When people started to figure out what was going on, then they owned up to it. As the world's people observe more strange trails in the sky, we begin to ask more questions that the government can't answer. As we ask more questions, the world governments push justification through the mainstream media and their scientific studies."

Aluminum spraying has contributed to autism in children, increased Alzheimer's disease in the elderly, the destruction of plants, trees, fish, birds, insects, and other forms of life. And most likely the great drought conditions in the Southwest, California, and throughout the world.

Chemtrail spraying has gone on since the late 1990s and continues. It only stopped shortly after the lockdown in 2020 when everyone was worried about the pandemic. Then on October 8, 2020, I noticed the sky over Southern Nevada was covered in chemtrails all day and into the late evening, and the next day the same weather pattern prevailed, yet not one chemtrail appeared in the sky. Can someone explain to me how that can happen?

Shame on those who want to control us, harm us, and this beautiful and very unique planet. Shame on those who continue to cover up this massive operation and claim that we are seeing only contrails in the sky, natural jet condensation. Their debunking is massive as the chemtrails, and they think we are all stupid. They are complicit in tyranny against humanity and our planet.

In time, they will be stopped, and the truth will be known. As the Bible states, "Ye will know the truth, and the truth shall set you free." John 8:32.

In 2022, I foresee another year of horrible wildfires throughout the world and again in northern and southern California, Oregon and Washington, Idaho, the rainforests in Brazil, and Australia. I urge any of you that live in forested areas to leave at the first sign of fires in your area. Grab only essentials and your pets and get out. The new wildfires are burning much hotter and faster, leaving little time to escape.

Betsey Lewis

The most reliable way to predict the future is to create it. —
Abraham Lincoln (1809-1865)

CHAPTER 18

MORE PREDICTIONS

1.   **TRUMP'S FUTURE**. I foresee Trump running for President again in 2024, but probably not winning. Trump's future as President in 2024 is nebulous at the moment and I doubt he will ever be president again. The Democrats will continue to try to dig up dirt on him about why he didn't try to stop the January 6 Capitol protests that turned violent or more Russian collusion—all fake news. He is also under investigation for tax fraud. Those close to him may sing to escape prosecution. In 2016, I accurately predicted Trump's presidential win seven months before he was elected in a powerful vision, but I got it wrong in 2020, and still believe the voting was not honest. I also predicted that President Trump would not be impeached the first and second time Congress tried to impeach Trump over fake claims of Russian collusion. It was just a witch hunt by the leftist Democrats. In 2024, Trump's numerology year will be ONE,

which means he will run for president again, and could be victorious. Again, events are changing, and I will foresee a clearer picture of Trump's destiny by 2023. However, Trump will be 79 years old in 2024, and his popularity may have greatly waned by then.

2. **JOE BIDEN**: For Biden, I foresee that he will most likely not complete his presidential term by 2024—either from dementia or some other means, including impeachment. If it doesn't happen in 2022, it will happen before 2024. It's going to be a bitter pill for people when they awaken to the deceit they've been handed about Biden and the unconscionable things he is doing to destroy America—such as allowing millions of illegal migrants to enter our country. Many are cartel members and vicious criminals entering our border and being bused or flown into major U.S. cities. Biden will go down in history as the worst President of the United States.

3. **MASSIVE SHORTAGES:** The truckers that we depend on to deliver our products to grocery stores and other major stores will impact us in Canada and the United States, walking off their jobs.

4. **PLANET X:** Planet X will be seen in front of the sun worldwide. As earth changes become more apparent in 2022, volcanoes awakening everywhere, mysterious booms, and powerful earthquakes are precursors to Earth's poles shifting. The New Madrid fault could happen this year with all the unusual earthquakes in South Carolina, Georgia, and Philadelphia.

5. **HARD TIMES:** I foresee hard times for people in the United States under the Biden administration, more freedom of speech will be taken from the American people, businesses will continue to close, unemployment numbers will rise, homeless people will continue to grow, drug abuse will sky rocket, lines of people hungry, illegals storming our borders and masses of people jobless due to COVID vaccine mandates. Who will the Democrats blame now for all the bad things that will happen in 2022? Certainly not themselves!

6. **MY PAST PREDICTIONS:** I predicted Prince Philip would die in 2021, about COVID and how it would kill millions, and I predicted Harry and Meghan Markle would marry and have a boy and a girl. I have predicted huge wildfires destroying homes, extreme weather in the summer, and extreme cold temperatures

in 2022. I predicted massive suicides of people giving up because of COVID as well as children committing suicide. I predicted volcanoes erupting and powerful earthquakes in 2021. I predicted in 2021 that World War III could happen anytime in the next three years, and how fast we would lose our freedom of speech and democracy. I predicted that famous people involved with the late Jeffrey Epstein will make shocking news and that Epstein was murdered (evidence now proves this). He didn't commit suicide. The rabbit hole goes deep, and now it has become news that Billionaire Bill Gates was known to be one of Epstein's buddies. Ghislaine Maxwell's fate could be like that of Jeffrey Epstein—murdered. She may not live to rat on the people involved. It will be uncovered that satanic rituals were involved.

7. **PEOPLE LEAVING IN 2022**: Actress and comedian Betty White passed on Dec. 31, 2021, before her 100th birthday on January 17. Many people have chosen to leave in huge numbers at this time and return when COVID and the threat of wars are gone on Earth, a long time from now. There is a gray aura around singer Celine Dion, and I fear her vibrational rate is extremely low at this time. Already, she has canceled concert dates because of an undisclosed illness. Her illness could be anorexia, an eating disorder.

South African leader Desmond Tutu, (1933-2021), was a longtime friend of his Holiness the Dalai Lama, now 86. Tutu and the 14th Dalai Lama were kindred souls, and his passing in 2021, might be the trigger for his Holiness to pass in 2022. Other famous spiritual or religious leaders in their 80s will pass as well. Ninety-five-year-old Queen Elizabeth's health is waning. I don't foresee her living beyond 2022. Prince Charles will take the throne!

Singer Tony Bennett, who suffers from Alzheimer's disease, will turn 96 on August 3, 2022, but I sense he will leave us either before or shortly after his birthday.

8. **CRIME AND DRUGS**: Thousands, especially the homeless, will die from COVID, Fentanyl crisis, and crime. Now that police have been defunded in many states, crime is escalating, and innocent people are being killed on the streets in broad daylight. Did you know that Beijing is fueling the fentanyl crisis in Canada and the United States through a sophisticated web involving drug cartels, loan sharks, and foreign casinos? It's right out of the Ozark television series. More than 100,000 people in the

United States died of drug overdoses from April 2020 to April 2021, a record number, according to the U.S. Centers for Disease Control and Prevention. Fentanyl was involved in nearly two-thirds of those deaths, and the numbers are going to rise. China doesn't need to launch a missile or invade our country—they already have through deadly drugs!

Beware of gathering in large places where you can be an easy target for a shooter. Schools should have better security for their children.

9. **KARMA AND RETURNING**: Maybe we should all rethink changing our ways and becoming more spiritual before we leave this planet because we will have to wait a few thousand years to reincarnate again due to Earth changes and fewer babies being born. We advance faster in physical bodies than in the spirit world. We are destroying ourselves and we are the only ones who will save us from our own destruction!

10. **FINANCIAL OUTLOOK FOR THE UNITED STATES AND THE WORLD.** I foresee the Stock Market falling many times through the year due to food and supply shortages, airline problems, 5G problems with airlines landing, and more news on future COVID variants. Although future variants will be less harmful, the Biden administration will make them more fearful. Please, if you are pregnant, do not get the vaccine. You will harm the fetus or have a miscarriage!

11. **CYBER WARS:** Expect major companies to be hacked by Russia or China. Our electrical grid is vulnerable too. I foresee a large outage across the U.S. in 2022.

12. **HUGE TAX INCREASES BY BIDEN**, thousands of illegals pouring into our country on the U.S. and Mexican border from China, Iran, Turkey, Mexico. Biden is giving everything free to these illegals crossing our borders, including homes and hotels at no cost. Inflation will escalate, people walking off jobs due to vaccine mandates, shortages, and more small businesses closing in 2022, a Master Number Year, will cause huge shortages. Our country will suffer from spiraling gas prices, food prices, heating prices, and everything else.

13. **MOVIE AND TELEVISION WILL RETURN SLOWLY,** but movie theaters will never recover completely from COVID. A large number of theaters will close permanently. The movie and television industry will see more layoffs. Las Vegas will be hit

hard again with closures and canceled concerts as singer Adele did recently.

14. **GROWING POLITICAL UNREST GLOBALLY**—riots, protests, violence, blood in the streets. I keep seeing a huge explosion in a European country like Ukraine or Mideast—perhaps nuclear. Russia is trying to stop Ukraine from becoming a member of NATO. Biden, Democrats, some Republicans, and the major media are fanning the flames of war. Humans on the move worldwide, escaping war, dictatorships, and cataclysms.

15. **THE U.S. WAS COMPLICIT IN SUPPORTING CHINA'S WUHAN Laboratory.** Dr. Fauci was involved as well. Fauci wants to go down in history as the COVID-19 vaccine savior. The question needs to be answered why the U.S. financed biological weapons with China, knowing that COVID was highly infectious? In my *2021 Looking into the Future* book on Amazon, I predicted this: "The release of this biological weapon was long-planned by the New World Order to destabilize our world. Did the Chinese mastermind the Coronavirus in their laboratories? Was it an accident? NO! The virus was well planned and ready to be released on the world in late 2019. Was it a way to cull the herd of Earth's 7.8 billion people?"

16. **GAS, HEATING, AND ANYTHING CONNECTED TO OIL** will skyrocket in 2022, now that Biden has halted oil production in the United States and the war in Ukraine. Everything including our groceries will skyrocket in price. Lumber prices will continue to soar and that may cause a run-on paper products again. Construction that was started on residential homes and commercial will be halted due to spiraling construction costs. Look to modular homes as the future of homes and commercial.

17. **REAL ESTATE WILL DO WELL** IN SOME AREAS IN THE UNITED STATES as the need for apartment rentals and cheaper housing continues. House prices will start to drop by early fall. But car prices will continue to rise including used cars. Modular homes will become popular and more affordable than stick-built.

18. **THE STOCK MARKET WILL BE A ROLLER COASTER**, and mostly down as Biden continues to give financial markets the jitters and the thought of interest rates rising three or four times this year. Cryptocurrencies will

continue to fall. There could be some kind of block or ban on cryptocurrencies in Canada and U.S.

19. **NANCY PELOSI, 81,** will step down as House Speaker in 2022. Nancy has been involved with insider trading and making millions as well as other Democrats and Republicans in Congress. In 2004, poor Martha Stewart was convicted on numerous felony charges, including conspiracy and making false statements to investigators looking into the sale of a stock, and served five months in a West Virginia federal prison camp for women, known as "Camp Cupcake," before serving another five at her home in New York. How can Pelosi and others get away with this without being convicted? The House of Cards will soon fall.

20. **WEATHER-RELATED DISASTERS** will dominate the news throughout the world—record-breaking cold, snow, torrential rains, tornadoes, hurricanes, flooding, and the summer of 2021 will continue to see extreme record-breaking heat, drought, and horrible wildfires. There will be torrential rains in Texas, scorching heat in the southwest, and continued drought conditions into 2024.

21. **MORE OF THE WORLD'S FREEDOM OF SPEECH** will vanish because of the censorship by social media and the news media owned by big corporations. The insanity will continue as more statues representing our past are removed, and beloved children's books banned. Our history is being rewritten by the cancel culture and the wokeness idiots.

22. **A SOLAR SUPERSTORM IN 2022** like the Carrington Event of Sept. 1-2, 1859, which was caused by a huge solar coronal mass ejection. The X-Class flare hit Earth's magnetosphere and induced the largest geomagnetic storm on record. A solar storm of this magnitude occurring today would cause widespread electrical disruptions, cell phone outages, blackouts, loss of GPS, and damage due to extended outages of the electrical grid. Satellites will go down and there will be massive communication disruptions for several days. Incredible fire-red auroras globally.

23. **STRANGE SIGHTINGS IN THE SKY:** UFOs will come in all sizes and shapes in 2022. Some UFOs are holographic inserts created to deceive us. Watch for mass sighting and probably a landing where officials can't deny it, but they will try and claim it was mass hypnosis. There are alien Stargates and

portals throughout the world. Utah's Skinwalker Ranch is one such place where aliens come and go, cattle are mutilated, and strange beings are seen. A major event by extraterrestrials will take place in 2022.

24. **GLACIERS MELTING:** Several huge glaciers will separate from Antarctica due to high temperatures this summer.

25. **MAJOR VOLCANIC ERUPTIONS WORLDWIDE,** and several undersea explosions producing Tsunamis like the Tonga eruption. Strong earthquakes will hit the Vatican in Rome, South Pacific, and along the U.S. West Coast. Washington, D.C. could see a strong earthquake again. Large earthquakes in California, off the coast of Oregon, Nevada, Hawaii, Alaska, and Japan. Possible megathrust 9.0 earthquakes along the Pacific Rim of Fire off the coast of Oregon and Washington and in the South Pacific in June or July.

26. **RUSSIA AND UKRAINE AND OUR BORDERS**: It's doubtful Russia will invade Ukraine until after the Winter Olympics in China as some have suggested. If Biden continues to interfere, things could heat up, especially if U.S. troops are sent in. Putin has become unstable and could attack with nuclear weapons. Why can't we protect our borders in the United States as over a million have entered our country illegally? Hungry has done it successfully without building an expensive wall. It will get worse as illegals throughout the world invade our country. Many are criminals, murders, and drug cartels here to kill U.S. citizens and bring in more drugs.

27. **MID-TERM ELECTIONS**. The Republicans will control the Democratic Congress in 2022, and the Senate will gain more Republicans. 34 Senate seats and all 435 House seats are up for election on November 8, 2022.

28. **UNITED KINGDOM** – Party animal, Prime Minister Boris Johnston will get the boot in late 2022. England will lower their strict COVID mandates as Omicron wanes and other countries will follow. Australia will finally halt its Draconian mandates and lockdowns as COVID becomes just the flu later in 2022 into 2023.

29. **CANADA:** The government of Canada has required COVID-19 vaccinations for approximately 268,000 federal public servants, including members of the Royal Canadian Mounted Police. Those government workers—including employees working remotely and contractors—had until Oct. 29, 2021 to

disclose their vaccination status. If you are 12 or older you must have proof, you were vaccinated to fly both domestic or international flights departing from airports in Canada. Justin Trudeau's mandates will get harsher in 2022. Truckers coming and going from Canada must have proof of the vaccine. Like the U.S., truckers will walk off their jobs and Canada's citizens will suffer from huge shortages.

30. **HOW SOCIAL MEDIA CONTROLS US AND OUR REALITY.** I urge you to watch *The Social Dilemma* on Netflix. The documentary is a huge wake-up call on how we are all being controlled by social media and mainstream news. In this documentary, former employees of Google, Facebook, and Twitter speak about why they left these companies and how their technology is used to gather information on us—everything about us—our likes and dislikes, what sites we visit daily, our friends, family, and what we buy. If that isn't scary enough, they use this to manipulate us. Again, read that last sentence. They know your life and how people have become addicted to the internet and social media. The algorithms watch us, and they push us into sites that support our beliefs—conspiracy theories, hate posts, leftist posts, etc. Social Media and the News Media use psychology against you! You are being controlled by them. You are a commodity to social media! It has become so horrific that humanity no longer interacts with each other, we don't know what the truth is—no one really knows anymore because the truth is so distorted. We distrust each other, we hate each other for their opposing beliefs, we have become more depressed, more violent, more hateful, and for what?

31. **SUICIDES WILL INCREASE AMONG CHILDREN AND ADULTS FROM COVID-19 LOCKDOWNS.** A great number of young people and adults have committed suicide since COVID-19 began in 2020. Mental health has been a persistent issue for people living through COVID. Not only has COVID put a strain on people who have pre-existing mental health conditions, but it has triggered mental health crises in the general population. Health anxiety, isolation, and a decrease in mental health services have all contributed to this increase in COVID-related emotional distress. If you know of anyone, reach out to them and tell them that life is going to get better. This is only a test that we all chose at this time. It's an incredible time to grow spiritually.

Some believe suicide means eternal hell and no redemption, but they are completely wrong. Suicides do not have any particular punishment, except for the soul's choosing. However, any problems that were not faced in this life will be faced in another. There are different reasons for suicide—such as those with terminal diseases and in extreme pain, depression, mental illness, and those running from their problems, which is the hardest lesson for that soul. Escaping life's problems and taking your life is wrong and a type of suicide that the soul may spend many lifetimes resolving.

If a person kills himself believing that the act will destroy his consciousness forever, then this false idea may severely impede his soul's progress and be intensified by guilt.

Remember the soul judges self, not God, so the soul has to either find forgiveness in self or torture self in their own created hell. As I said before, the Creator or God, does not judge us, never has, and never will. Those who commit suicide to stop endless pain from a terminal illness, or accidentally die from a drug overdose, will find forgiveness faster on the Other Side than those who run from their problems and commit this act. Prayers of love and forgiveness are always needed for these souls.

In Jane Robert's channeled book. *The Seth Material*, Jane was told by Seth, an ancient teacher, that after a suicide, teachers are available to explain the true situation. Various therapies are used. For example, the personality may be led back to the events before the decision. Then the personality is allowed to change the decision. An amnesia effect is induced so that the suicide itself is forgotten. Only later is the individual informed of the act, when he is better able to face it and understand it. Sometimes the personality refuses to accept the face of death. The individual knows quite well that he is dead on your terms, but he refuses to complete the psychic separation. Now: There are instances of course where the individuals concerned do not realize the fact of death. It is not a matter of refusing to accept it, but a lack of perception. In this state, such an individual will also be obsessed with earthly concerns and wander perhaps bewildered throughout his home or surroundings.

Unfortunately, there are a huge number of souls trapped in this reality, and someday when humans have learned how to clear the ethereal band surrounding Earth, these lost souls will be released from their self-imposed prison.

Seth continued: Those who understand thoroughly that reality is self-created will have the least difficulty [on the Other Side]. Those who have learned to understand and operate the mechanics of the dream state will have a great advantage. A belief in demons is highly disadvantageous after death, as it is during physical existence. A systematized theology of opposites is also detrimental. If you believe, for example, that all good must be balanced by evil, then you bind yourself into a system of reality that is highly limiting, and that contains within it the seed of great torment.

32. **COVID:** The Covid virus will never vanish, but it will become less virulent on the population as the Spanish Flu did from 1918 to 1920. Omicron is killing people, both vaccinated and unvaccinated, and those who are obese or ill. Eventually, humanity will get back to normal again, but President Biden and his minion of Democratic followers will continue to put fear in those who don't conform to vaccination mandates. There will be more variants, but not as harmful as the original COVID-19 and Delta variant. I fear there will be side effects for people who received the vaccines in years to come, and also for children. Again, I suggest Ivermectin for anyone sick with COVID by having a doctor prescribe it. Most hospitals will not administer it. Also, you will need to find a compounding pharmacy to fill the prescription. Major pharmacies refuse to fill Ivermectin prescriptions. Hospitals are becoming places of death, not life, and they refuse to administer life-saving drugs that have proven to help. Recently, monoclonal treatments were banned by the FDA. That's evil!

34. **LABORATORIES CONTINUE TO CONDUCT HORRIBLE EXPERIMENTS** on animals—monkeys and dogs. On January 24, 2022, a truck crashed on a Pennsylvania highway carrying one hundred monkeys to a laboratory. It sparked fear that the monkey was infected with something extremely virulent. Certain agencies killed the monkeys and people were told to stay away. A woman who came in contact with one that escaped was warned it might have a deadly disease. The test monkeys were on their way to a laboratory in Florida when the truck crashed into a garbage truck on Friday near Danville, Pennsylvania, with four of the primates escaping.

No one has explained why the monkeys, if infected with something dangerous, were being transported to Florida. Why is the U.S. still involved in inhumane experiments on animals? Peta recently uncovered the abuse of beagle dogs in Virginia. Five thousand were sold to a laboratory in Virginia for medical research.

35. **NEXT SUPREME COURT JUSTICE**: Justice Stephen Breyer is retired, and President Biden can't wait to have a black woman replace his seat on the Supreme Court. Sadly, other nationalities won't be considered for the position. Biden's nominee for Supreme Nominee is Federal Justice Katanji Brown Jackson, a black woman. I don't see her being nominated due to leniency for child pornography offenders and child pedophiles. She couldn't definite what is a woman during the hearings.

36. **INTEREST RATES** will be raised four times this year. Inflation will continue to rise above 8%. Recession headed our way.

37. **ON JANUARY 27, 2022, TRUCKERS HEADED TO OTTAWA** to protest the Canadian government's COVID-19 vaccine mandate for cross-border drivers. Several thousand people greeted them along the way on Friday, January 28. This is just the beginning of people tired of the tyranny and control of our leaders. How did they suddenly transform into "evil-doers" within two years? Expect more protests and rallies across Canada, the United States, Australia, New Zealand, and Europe. Prime Minister Trudeau will do everything to shut the Truckers down, including a freeze on their bank accounts. This could happen in the U.S. by March.

38. **MORE FALLING BRIDGES:** On January 28, 2022, a bridge in Pittsburg, PA fell, injuring 10 people. Luckily, no one was killed. Biden visited Pittsburg earlier in the day to support his infrastructure bill. He promised to get all bridges fixed this year, but don't hold your breath. At least three bridges will fall this year. Bridges will be in the news in 2022—relating to truckers.

39. **U.S. BORDERS:** It is estimated that 2 million illegals have crossed the U.S. borders and have been flown or bussed into major cities. Biden has given them money, housing and health care, but many are men coming in without families. They are coming in from China, Mideast, South America, and Mexico, and a large number have criminal records. Between 1788 and 1868, 162,000 convicts from Britain and Ireland were sent to Australia to various penal colonies. The United States of America is

becoming a criminal country. Expect crime to skyrocket—murders, rapes, looting, and terrorist attacks on innocent people. Please stay away from large gatherings as much as possible.

Recently Biden announced 100,000 Ukrainian refugees will be allowed into the United States. What will these people do to support themselves if the United States doesn't?

40. **WORLD WAR III:** If WWIII happens this year or next, it will be started by Russian President Vladimir Putin who has plans to invade other countries. Nuclear weapon could be used if he thinks he's losing ground in Ukraine. This will begin WWIII. Pray it doesn't happen. Also, I predict that China will move on Taiwan and North Korea will launch a missile perhaps at South Korea. Chaotic world in 2022.

41. **HUGE SHORTAGES WORLDWIDE:** With the sanctions in Russia, the world will experience vast shortages in food, wheat, oil, gas. Biden has already warned of global food shortages as Russia-Ukraine war upends wheat supplies. Biden warns of global food shortages as Russia-Ukraine war upends wheat supplies.

THE FUTURE IS CONSTANTLY FORMING and changing. The future is not set in stone. The above predictions I've provided are only probabilities in space and time and the future can be changed by mass consciousness if everyone gets on the same page. We create our reality on a personal level and through global mass consciousness. Our fear is creating our world, and it is up to us to change it. We affect everything around us with our actions, thoughts, and words—even earthquakes and solar events. Humans have forgotten how we are connected to each other and nature, and until we understand this truth our world will continue to be chaotic and violent. Let's create a kinder, more compassionate, and loving world instead of hating each other for our differences. We are all made by the same benevolent being and we should honor everyone and everything.

Earth is in dire straits at this time. You are asked to step up and be renegades standing up for your beliefs that others may not support. This is not a time for the weak. The problem at this time is that we believe we are separate from all energy that is around us. We have separated ourselves from the whole.

Earth is a classroom, and you are the students. In school, there were those eager to learn and there were the slackers. It's not your place to recruit the slackers who stick their heads in the sand and refuse to get off the couch and make changes. They expect someone to do it for them.

It is time for you to commit to create a reality of love, joy, compassion for yourself. Only then will you help others, for if you do not evolve yourself, you do not serve others. Become the example, by following your heart, trusting your intuition, and you will teach others to follow with courage.

Betsey Lewis

CHAPTER 19

EXTRATERRESTRIALS AMONG US

Humanity has been an experiment. Aliens have created many worlds, lifeforms, and terra-formed planets. Prime Creator or God gave them as well as us the ability to be co-creators in the Universe. But the creator god's plan got out of control. According to the Pleiadians in Barbara Marciniak's book, *Bringers of the Dawn,* the plan came together to design Earth as an intergalactic exchange center of information. Earth was a beautiful place, located on the fringes of one of the galactic systems and easily reached from other galaxies. It was close to many portals or Stargates, highways that exist for energies to travel throughout space.

There was much hurrying and shuffling to create individual representation from all the galaxies here upon this planet. Some of the creator gods were and are master geneticists. They were able through their hierarchies to tie molecules together—encoded molecules of identity, frequency, and electrical charge, to create life. Many sentient civilizations gave their DNA to have representation of their coding upon Earth. The master geneticists then designed various species, some humans, some animals, by playing with the varieties of DNA donated by sentient civilizations to make Earth the center of information exchange. Earth became a center of information, a light center, and a Living Library. The plan was a grand one.

The Original Planners of Earth were members of the Family of Light, beings who worked for and were associated with an aspect of consciousness called Light. Light is information. Earth was supposed to be a wondrous place of Light and information where knowledge was shared.

Different energies were brought into existence here. There were species of humans on Earth around 500,000 years ago who developed into highly evolved civilizations. This is before Lemuria and Atlantis. These civilizations are buried under the ice caps on the far southern continent of Antarctica. Lately, Google Earth has captured what looks like remnants of an advanced civilization in Antarctica.

Of course, in time, the project of the Living Library on Earth was fought over. There were wars in space. Read the ancient Sanskrit texts, dated back over 4,000 B.C. that describe wars in space. The Ramayana even describes a beautiful chariot that 'arrived shining, a wonderful divine car that sped through the air.' In another passage, there is mention of a chariot being seen 'sailing overhead like a moon.' In the Mahabharata the stories are no less astounding: "Bhima flew with his Vimana on an enormous ray which was as brilliant as the sun and made a noise like the thunder of a storm."

Who owns the Earth? Many species of extraterrestrials. Some of the creator gods took advantage of the free-will zone on Earth and did whatever they wanted. These beings raided earth 300,000 years ago, the beginning of what we call "modern homo sapiens."

The ETs that won the fight, did not want humans to be informed of what had taken place because we would be easier to control. That is why Light is information and Dark is lack of information. Earth was inundated with radiation and nuclear action from the ETs warring against each other to control us. These beings were also master geneticists and knew how to create a plethora of life.

These beings also learned how Prime Creator or God created

an electromagnetic frequency of consciousness as a food source for self. The new owners who came to Earth 300,000 years ago were the ones spoken of in the Bible, in the Babylonian and Sumerian tablets, and all texts throughout the world.

We have borders around countries, but there were borders around the planet to control how much the frequencies of humans could be modulated and changed. We are the Family of Light and need to be triggered again to hold that Light. When human DNA begins to rebundle as a twelve-stranded helix system and this information is acted upon, there will be incredible power within us.

Simply by coming together and intending what we want— jointly becoming a telepathic receptacle for energies from all over the cosmos—will change the face of the Universe.

The Family of Dark are creator gods who are uninformed about the true meaning of the Universe and Prime Creator. They are the reptilian species or "Lizzies." They reside underground in deep bases and caverns worldwide, and like to experiment on humans and other life. They watch us and know everything we are doing on top of the Earth. The funny thing is that most of you have been extraterrestrials in past lives. You don't keep returning to Earth but experience many lives in the Universe.

There are blue beings, Nordics that look human, insect beings, bird beings, and many types of grays. Just like humans, there is a benevolent Lizzie population and those who are dark and malevolent. Some work with our governments.

Humans must realize how complex reality is, how many different forms of reality there are, and how we are all connected to the same God-consciousness. The creator gods have been drawn back here at this time because of the Divine Plan. This year, 2022, will shock all of you about the reality of nature and on extraterrestrials. A major event is coming, and it will be a great unveiling.

During the 1950s and 1960s, the majority of people were skeptical about the existence of aliens because the military and government wanted the truth debunked about the growing UFO sightings. Astronomer J. Allen Hynek (1910-1986) was hired to be the military's advisor on Project Sign (1947-1949), and Project Blue Book (1952-1969). At first, Hynek dismissed reports as logical explanations as people confusing a UFO with the planet Venus, swamp gas, and other ridiculous explanations.

Project Blue Book was the code name for an Air Force program set up in 1952, after numerous UFO sightings during the Cold War era, to explain away or debunk as many reports as possible to mitigate possible panic and shield the public from a genuine national security problem—a technological phenomenon that was beyond human control and was not Russian, and yet represented an unfathomable potential threat.

On Friday, June 25, 2021, the Office of the Director of National Intelligence (ODNI) released its eagerly awaited unclassified intelligent report, titled, "Preliminary Assessment: Unidentified Aerial Phenomena" or UAP. The document was a disappointment to the UFO community with its brief nine-page version of a much larger classified report provided to the Congressional Services and Armed Services Committees. The report withheld specific details of its data sample, which consisted of 144 UFO reports made mainly by military pilots between 2004 and 2021. They concluded that "a handful of UAPs appeared to demonstrate advanced technology."

The military rebranded unidentified flying objects (UFOs) as UAP, in part, to avoid the stigma that was attached to alien claims visiting Earth since the Roswell crash in 1947.

The debunkers of UFOs believe that the Navy has experienced top-secret, advanced Chinese or Russian aircraft in the United States airspace. Their technology far exceeds anything humanly possible. But no one can answer why a UAP can enter large bodies of water at high speeds without breaking up and then dive beneath the ocean until it vanishes. If any human being piloted a UFO and entered the water at those speeds, they would turn to mush. No country on Earth has that kind of technology at this time.

Swarms of flashing "Tic Tac" shaped UFOs have chased four U.S. Navy destroyers and hovered above them for weeks, ship logs revealed. These mysterious and unidentified objects have chased Naval ships for up to 100 nautical miles off the coast of California. It's a known fact that UFOs have been spotted off the coast of Southern California and around the Catalina Island area for over fifty years now.

In my 2021 book, *Stargates—ET Undersea and Underground Bases Revealed*, I have revealed portals used by these beings to travel instantly from place to place, and where their bases reside throughout. The truth is our military does not want humanity to know that different beings reside in our oceans and underground in massive bases, and they have been here for thousands or millions of years. They have abducted millions of humans to experiment on us.

Undersea or Underground Beings

Are the so-called aliens that have bases under the sea and underground throughout the world the same beings or are they different species? From what I have researched, they are different beings that occupy the underground world than the ones under our oceans and deepest lakes.

The characteristic of a normal reptile is a land dweller. Most of the reports from abductees are the grays answer to the Lizzie population and do their bidding, while undersea beings and those that reside in deep lakes like Russia's Lake Baikal are different species than the reptilians.

Renowned abductee Betty Andreasson Luca has always maintained that her encounters were with benevolent beings or angels. The tiny grays appeared to be more robotic than the human-looking Elders in their white robes. At one point, Betty described the tall, white-haired Elders in a strange mystical ceremony that involved moving energy.

The three elders walked over to a round design on the floor and stood within it, forming a triangle. Then each one stretched out their arms to each other, touching hands palm to palm with their fingers pointed upward. They each bowed their heads in reverence.

Betty stood beside another Elder watching the ceremony in bewilderment as a ring of light formed in the middle of the three Elders. The light was coming out of their foreheads as they touched each other's foreheads, forming a triangle. Four more Elders joined the original group with hands pointed upward and bowing.

At that point, a ring of light formed around them, as they began to chant "Oh, Oh, Oh, Oh, in low voices. Two V-shaped beams of light burst from their foreheads and formed a six-pointed star with a smaller ring of light in its center.

Figure 32. Elders chanting around globe of light

Elders chanting around a globe of light

In another adventure, Betty watched as aging Elders in black robes and the smaller Watchers were led down a hall. Betty asked why there were no women and was told, "We are neither male nor female here. Humans are male and female, and the male is the dominant one." Betty then asked, "Well, what am I doing here then?" The alien's response was, "Don't you remember your blessing? Betty didn't understand what he meant.

Betty learned that the small grays needed their biobics (eyes) replaced from time to time because their natural eyes wear out. New biobics are then given to them.

In another abduction, Betty was transported to a hospital room where an elderly man lay in bed dying. A dark entity and light entity were fighting to gain control of what Betty perceived was his soul. The scene reminded me of the 1990 movie, *Ghost,* starring Patrick Swayze and Demi Moore, where dark entities come for the bad guy, played by Tony Goldwyn, who murders the Swayze character, Sam Wheat.

The little gray Watchers told Betty, "We are the Gardeners, and the gardener has to remove dead wood, he has to pluck unwanted weeds. Our history goes back billions of years of Earth time. Man is so new upon the Earth that no human has the right to even attempt to judge what we do...We must ensure that the works of Man do not pollute Space and endanger other worlds...Our purpose is to save your world. To save it from what threatens to be suicide. To save it from utter pollution. New weapons will be developed. Man will enter space within the next hundred years. Thus, it is that we are interested."

What they told Betty sounds arrogant, as if they created us and own us, and maybe they do. Perhaps Betty was shown holographic images of beings that don't exist, while the real aliens or terrestrial beings operate the controls behind the curtain like the *Wizard of Oz*. Or were the Elders clones created by other beings?

Preston Dennett wrote the book, *The Healing Power of UFOs*, which cataloged over 300 true accounts of people healed by extraterrestrials. He added this caveat, "It's not all rainbows and lollipops. Many experiencers have suffered medically as a result of their encounters and have not been healed. Other experiencers suffer from naturally occurring human diseases and injuries, and they are not being healed. And even those who have been healed sometimes experience injuries or mental and emotional trauma due to their encounters."

Some experiencers, he said, admit to being healed, but believe that their treatment at the hands of ETs is little different than how humans treat lab rats. They feel that the cures are not done out of kindness or pity but are motivated by the aliens; selfish desires to keep their human experiments healthy, only to ensure the successful production of hybrid babies and the ETs pursuit of knowledge of the human form.

If they can cure us as Lisa's mother claimed from her abduction with the red-headed ETs when she was taken to what appeared a laboratory full of vials (included in another chapter), why aren't they helping us? They always dangle the proverbial carrot in front of us.

Can you imagine if extraterrestrials cured all of humanity's diseases instantly? Imagine the consequences. No one dying for years and the result of over-population which we currently have. As Preston Dennett wrote, "And just think what would happen if our military leaders were given healing technology from the aliens. The ability to cure flesh wounds in seconds would only give warring countries a never-ending supply of soldiers. Or what if the technology was available only to the wealthy? In all likelihood, the consequences would be worse."

And think of the billions and billions of dollars the pharmaceutical companies would lose. They won't let that happen.

It feels as if a turning point is going to take place soon and we are going to experience a new generation of hybrid children and adults entering our world. Will it be after some catastrophic natural event or a created event that will wipe out millions of humans besides COVID-19? Will a war between ETs take place to gain complete control of our planet as they did eons ago according to ancient Indian texts?

Clones versus Real Human

Can we assume that the stories Dr. Ardy Sixkiller Clarke heard from Native Americans about cloned humans unloaded from ET craft on Indian reservations and driven to U.S. cities are true? If so, how many clones are walking around our cities—thousands or millions and are the the ones that are changing our world for the worst creating anger, violence, and rioting in cities?

And what happened to the ones they originally took the clone from? One Native American claimed he witnessed his own clone or avatar leave a UFO. His identical clone appeared clumsy and not very knowledgeable about human behavior. Have the clones infected our governments and religious organizations and what is their ultimate agenda in our world?

Portals and Stargates

There are stories about people vanishing in front of witnesses. UFOs have been seen in the sky and vanish instantly as if entering a portal or stargate. Are these natural to the planet? Perhaps, but I imagine some are created. If we access these portals, like the ETs, it would be like the theory of wormholes in space. A wormhole is a speculative structure linking disparate points in spacetime and is based on a special solution of the Einstein field equations. Scientists believe that wormholes could propel a spacecraft to the outer reach of the Cosmos almost instantly.

Some scientists have conjectured that if one mouth of a wormhole is moved in a specific manner, it could allow for time travel. Some of the so-called ETs might be time travelers. I have always believed in time travel—either traveling into the past or to the future. I do not doubt that someday we will time travel. Could we change history? I wonder if ETs have been altering our reality for eons, and sense they have.

Extraterrestrials seeded Earth
A theory published in the well-respected journal, *Progress in Biophysics and Molecular Biology,* in 2018 stated that life on Earth had its genetic code altered many times by extraterrestrial microscopic life and possibly even directly seeded with extraterrestrial embryos. While the paper, *Cause of the Cambrian Explosion—Terrestrial or Cosmic,* explores the mysterious origin of life on our planet that life began as a result of retroviruses that fell from space through meteorites and comets. The scientists theorized that the sudden evolution of squids and octopuses in Earth's oceans had extraterrestrial help as well as the evolution of humans and other species.

They asserted that instead of a gradual seeding of life here, some big event occurred, based on the magnitude of evolutionary change.

Is there a threat by some ETs?
If the Chinese, Russia, or North Korea tried to launch a live supersonic or nuclear missile at the United States or any other country, the ETs would react. They are watching closely what the Navy is doing on the East and West Coasts of the United States, and they are aware of Russia's, Iran's, China's, and North Korea's nuclear capabilities at this time. In Vietnam, U.S. military ships were fired on and there were casualties onboard. The U.S. military fired first on UFOs in Vietnam, and they retaliated. If they wanted to get rid of us, they could have done it eons ago. They can extinguish us in an instant.

An astrologer friend has been given visions of an alien invasion for 2022. I do not share this vision, and if something like that happen it will be a false flag event created by humans, not aliens.

The Coming Agenda in 2022
2022 will impact humanity as UFOs and their ships and orbs make massive appearances in our skies with more human contact. I sense they are going to make a grand appearance over a major city again as they did over Phoenix, Arizona on March 13, 1997. The cover-up will finally collapse as it is starting to do now, and the movement will only grow as more and more military personnel and scientists come forward about the ET presence on Earth.

I'd rather believe there are benevolent beings who think we are worth saving and want us to awaken to the tyranny of our world that has endured for thousands of years by the controlling ones.

This will be the beginning of a beautiful new world when we discover we are also Creator Gods—learning, growing, and evolving along with other advanced civilizations!

The plight of the non-Indian world is that it has lost respect for Mother Earth, from whom and where we all come. —Ed McGaa "Eagle Man" Oglala Sioux Ceremonial Leader

CHAPTER 20

HONORING EARTH AND ALL LIFE

Indigenous people worldwide have foreseen the coming changes for many decades and tell us the changes will herald a new Earth. They tell us we must return to the natural way of living as Earthkeepers as they practiced thousands of years ago. Once we do, our planet will return to balance—*ayni*. Although there are a great number of spiritually evolved people on the planet at this time, we haven't reached a total awakening. The indigenous people see a time we will be forced to awaken from our slumber and return to ancient wisdom by Earth changes.

The Hopi, the Inca, and other indigenous shamans speak of a purification time when Earth will turn or flip on its axis. An Andrean prophecy foretells of a period of transformation, when the Condor and the Eagle align, and a time of cosmic overturning of time and space that will signal the end of an era. This will be a time of humanity raising their consciousness and a new beginning. There will be a new relationship with Mother Earth and a Golden Age.

During this time of purification, many will choose to leave, and those who do remain will find new ways to live in harmony and gratitude with our Mother. The new children coming into the world now are old souls who are reincarnating very quickly, sensing they have an important role in the coming changes. These children bring a higher vibrational rate with them and enhanced psychic gifts—for they are the *newly evolved humans*.

This book is about honoring Mother Earth and all things on Earth. It's about returning to a simpler life, a more spiritual life, a more compassionate life, and a more caring life. By incorporating the lessons and knowledge, both ancient and indigenous inside this book, you will be on your way to creating a new future, and a new world. When we reconnect with the Living Library of Mother Earth, we connect to the mysteries, the age-old secrets of spirit beings that watch and guide our planet. The shamans, the elders, the holy men, and women practiced ceremonies for ages connecting to these benevolent beings that exist in the elements of our world. When we stop destroying the elements—Earth, Wind, Fire, Air, Water, and become balanced with these spirit beings, we'll discover that we can communicate with them. We will be aware of nature's signs and warnings.

Native teachings are based on Earth law and Nature herself. They teach us that everything is alive and has consciousness, even rocks, and all the elements are associated with dimensional beings like fairies, gnomes, angels. In our modern world, most of us have forgotten there is a transcendental world that is as real as the physical world, but we are so immersed in our material world we have forgotten the ethereal world. Also, as we destroy the elements, we are destroying ourselves.

The Lakota people have a phrase, *Mitakuye Oyasin,* which means, we are related to all things. The Lakota people, indigenous people, and the ancient ones have always seen the interconnectedness of all life on Mother Earth. It is the oneness of prayer and respect for all forms of life: people, the four-legged animals, trees, rivers, finned creatures, winged creatures, rocks, mountains, and valleys.

Ancient people understood Earth's uniqueness, how everything existed in perfect balance and how everything was connected to spirit. But today when we start harming, changing, and destroying the elements through our egos, everything becomes unbalanced and chaotic. Ancient people knew the elements not only existed outside us but within us. We are ONE with the cosmos. To honor Mother Earth, they practiced sacred ceremonies and called on the elements to guide them and protect them. Nothing was taken for granted.

Fast forward to the present day. Our planet suffers from unconscionable abuse and neglect. There are currently 7.2 billion humans living on Earth, and most of the billions of souls on Earth have forgotten their role as Earthkeepers and how exceptional and precious our planet is in the Solar System. We now stand at a precipice where we can either take action and heal our planet or watch our oceans, lakes, and rivers die, species vanish, and all our natural resources disappear. We are running out of time to repair the damage the collective "we" have unleashed on the planet in the last hundred years.

Maya Grandmother Flordemayo, one of the elders of the International Council of Thirteen Indigenous Grandmothers, said it best in *Grandmothers Counsel the World,* authored by Carol Schaefer, "To think that in a hundred years, we've lost total consciousness of everything. We, humans, have disrespected so much that in this time of movement, where the celestial doors have opened and heavenly beings are coming from the four directions to help us, but if we don't do what we've been asked to do, well...the results will be sad. We must learn how to wake up and stay awake during these dark and changing times."

Many of the worldwide environmental changes were foretold in native prophecy have already come to pass: the greenhouse effect, extreme changes in the seasons and in the weather, famine, disease, the disappearance of wildlife, and the hole in the ozone layer that native people refer to as "the hole in our lodging."

Another member of the Thirteen Indigenous Grandmothers, Grandmother Clara of the Amazon, spoke of her visit with the Star Beings. "Humanity and the Earth are being cleansed of the accumulated negativity caused by humanity's greater orientation to the material world and to technology, which has caused us to lose our connection to the Spirit World and nature. We are destroying our planet and ourselves as a result of our materialism. Since nature is the source of our visions and centers us in Truth, the more we destroy nature, the less able we are to live in balance and wisdom and the more wars, disease, and disharmony we create."

I do not consider myself a shaman in any sense; I'm certainly not indigenous, nor do I have all the answers, but I do consider myself an Earthkeeper and continue to do my best to heal our planet in ceremony and prayer. I discovered the miracle of nature at an early age while growing up in rural southwestern Idaho. For me, nature was alive in everything—the rocks, the rivers, lakes, mountains, wind, weather, trees, and all creatures indigenous to Idaho and the Northwest. Mother Earth was my teacher, and I was a student eager to learn about her. I'm not sure where this knowledge came from, but it was always there from my earliest memories. Having parents, who loved the wilderness, camping, hunting, and mining, certainly enhanced my love of the environment.

Of course, at the time I was much too young to understand that everything on our planet has a consciousness, even rocks, but I sensed the importance of nature. A river, a pond, a lake, and the mighty ocean, all have their own distinct voice and spirit. And like humans, the elements have their own personalities and moods—a placid lake can transform into angry waves, the ocean can produce tsunami waves, and a river that once flowed quietly through a valley can become raging water destroying everything in its path.

During the 1950s, my parents spent summers in the Northern Nevada desert where my grandfather owned mining property. In the wilderness areas of Idaho, I observed deer, bobcats, jack rabbits, ground squirrels, and all kinds of birds. Years later my parents purchased Dierkes Lake, a mile-long spring-fed lake in the Snake River Canyon of Southern Idaho, formed by a collapsed lava tube. Originally the lake had been an apple orchard during the turn of the twentieth century until spring water began bubbling up from the ground and pouring into the valley basin. Ten years later a lake had formed, one mile long and one hundred feet deep.

The lake was a magical place for my younger sister Kathy and me, where we lived in the water during the summer months—swimming, diving off rocks, water skiing, and boating. We rode our horses, fished, hiked to the upper crater lakes and assisted our parents in the concession stand, collecting the entrance fee and selling soda and candy. Our animal family consisted of three Siamese cats, several dogs, three horses, chickens, and a few sheep. The Lake's wildlife consisted of porcupines, rock chucks, coyotes, birds, ducks, geese, rabbits, snakes, and an occasional swan.

My only escape from turbulent family life was hiking alone to an upper lake, swimming in a secluded part of the lake, or sitting on a large granite boulder listening to the birds and watching the clouds pass by. Water was cathartic for me. Whenever I sought my private world of nature, I spoke to nature and God—because I could see God's creation in everything. I soon learned water had consciousness and a personality. On some days the lake was still and reflective as a mirror, but then a storm could quickly transform the water into angry white caps. Growing up in this wondrous environment taught me that everything is alive and full of energy.

Today, I never imagined Earth's natural resources would be destroyed at such an alarming rate as it has in the last fifty-plus years. What will future generations see and experience on Mother Earth? Certainly not the beautiful Earth I experienced during the fifties and sixties. The utter lack of regard for Mother Earth and her creatures always brings me to tears.

We are seeing more Earth changes and as we enter a window of increased activity, it's imperative we trust our intuition, the animals, and Mother Earth to warn us. When we learn to trust Mother Earth and her warnings, we are using Earth Wisdom practiced by ancient people and indigenous people globally.

Mother Earth showed her fierceness on December 26, 2004, from an undersea megathrust earthquake and subsequent tsunami off the coast of Sumatra, Indonesia that resulted in the deaths of 230,000 people in fourteen countries. The Native people in the outer islands understood nature and sensed this event before it happened. They managed not to suffer any fatalities as the mainlander people suffered. Even wild and domestic animals seemed to sense what was about to happen and fled to safety. According to eyewitnesses, elephants screamed and ran for higher ground, dogs refused to go outdoors, flamingos abandoned their low-lying breeding areas and zoo animals rushed into their shelters and could not be enticed to come back out.

On April 20, 2010, following the explosion and sinking of BP's Deepwater Horizon oil rig that took eleven lives. Oil began gushing from the site into the Gulf of Mexico. It is estimated 4.9

million barrels of oil flowed into the Gulf for 87 days. Subsequent attempts to harness the oil with toxic dispersants failed and resulted in the death of thousands of fish, shrimp, and other sea creatures, and the deaths of countless birds and wildlife.

The big oil companies still haven't learned their lesson from the largest accidental marine oil spill in the history of the petroleum industry. Deep water oil drilling continues worldwide, endangering wildlife, ocean life, and human life. It will continue happening like recent oil spills along the Southern California coast.

Another catastrophic Earth event occurred on Friday, March 11, 2011, when Japan experienced a 9.0 megathrust earthquake that lasted six minutes, followed by a powerful tsunami that reached heights of up to 40.5 meters (133 ft.) in Miyako and which, in the Sendai area, traveled up to 6 miles inland. The earthquake moved Honshu (the main island of Japan (8 ft.) east and shifted the Earth on its axis by estimates of between 4 inches and 10 inches. An estimated 20,000 people died that day.

Fukushima Daiichi nuclear disaster resulted when the plant was hit by a tsunami when a meltdown occurred in three of the plant's six nuclear reactors. The rate at which contaminated water has been estimated at 300 tons a day a few months after the disaster, and there are conflicting reports of the current flow.

Humanities foolishness toward Mother Earth rages on, and now fracking may be to blame for hundreds of swarm earthquakes hitting central Oklahoma, Kansas, Arizona, New Mexico, Texas, and southeastern Oregon, places not known for earthquake activity. As our planet experiences catastrophic weather, droughts, wildfires, powerful earthquakes, tsunamis, disastrous floods, catastrophic hurricanes like Katrina in New Orleans (2005) and Sandy (2012), and devastating tornadoes, we should understand that Mother Earth won't allow our abuse and disregard any longer. She wants to survive despite our destructive ways, and she is fighting back. Something inexplicable is happening to our planet.

From Russia to Australia, from Chile to the Eastern Coast of the United States, people are reporting these sounds. People are asking if these are warnings of a catastrophic Earth event approaching. These harmonics may signal a massive Earth core slippage or the total shift of the Earth's poles. Speculation is

Earth's liquid core is spinning at a different rate than the planet's rotation and the slippage is causing the migration of the Earth's magnetic field.

Although some conspiracy theorists suggest sky quakes are a product of the military's top-secret High-Frequency Active Auroral Research Program (HAARP) located in Gakona, Alaska, others believe the harmonics are from deep within the Earth traveling from a mutating core through the layers of the planet to the surface. The sky acts as a sounding board capturing and magnifying the sonic and electric frequencies shot from the center of Earth. The flashes of light are a product of piezoelectricity, created when rocks deep within the Earth begin to grind together under extreme stress.

Earth hasn't always been a peaceful place. Millions of years ago Earth was consumed in transformation where seas suddenly rose, islands disappeared, continents moved and flooded, volcanoes unleashed their furry, and mighty mountain ranges like the Andes and Himalayas rocketed from the depths of the ocean reaching many thousands of feet in the air within a matter of hours. Much of the United States was once covered in water and ancient seas. Today fossils and seashells can be found from North America to South America's jagged mountain peaks.

Rocks with Earth's crust contain crystals. It is known that before an earthquake the stored strain of energy is released as the fault slips and rocks return to their unstrained state and "earthquake lights" are produced. This appears to be happening everywhere but without the earthquakes. Slipping strata with the bowels of the planet create incredible pressures so great that temperatures soar and metals flow like liquids. Water in the Earth becomes superheated plasma and interacts with layers of quartz crystals emitting harmonics audible as a hum, boom, or moan creating Earth lights and sky quakes echoing across the sky. Earthquake lights were reported in the sky before the Fukushima earthquake in Japan in 2011, the 1971 Southern California earthquake, and as far back as the 1906 San Francisco earthquake.

Instead of fearing Mother Earth's changes, if we reconnect to her, we will understand the signs and warnings when she is about to move our world in a big way. That's how ancient ingenious people survived for thousands of years; by trusting their innate sixth sense—that forewarned them of earthquakes, storms, floods, warring tribes, and fierce animals.

We can no longer ignore Mother Earth's warnings. Prophecies speak of the cleansing that will take place by volcanoes, floods, famines, disease, the disappearance of wildlife, the greenhouse effect, and changes in the seasons. This book was written so that we—humanity will return to ancient wisdom and become Earthkeepers, Wisdomkeepers, and Rainbow Warriors again—that we will return to the natural way of Earth living—respecting and honoring everything. That we will understand the signs in the sky, the water, and in the creatures of Earth when our planet begins to move us. It is in this mindfulness that we emerge into Mother Earth and become One with Life.

Indigenous people believe that what we do today, at this moment, will affect the next seven generations, and so it is our responsibility to teach the children these sacred lessons about Mother Earth's Living Library, so they will continue the healing lineage of the Ancient Ones that came before us. When humans no longer feel they are superior above all life, when the human ego is no longer in command, then peace, balance, and harmony will reign on Earth.

My time with Indigenous mentors, and my visions are to offer hope, not fear, where the essence of respect, love, and pure heart manifests in all humans and is practiced daily. When we awaken to our relationship to the cosmos and Earth Wisdom, life will return to *ayni—balance.*

Why can't we honor all life? There's only one planet in this solar system with oceans, trees, and millions of plants, insects, sea creatures, and land creatures. We've lost sight of Earth's mysteries and magic. I see more of God in animals and all forms of life on Earth than in human beings.

Animals have every right to be here and treated well and many of earth animals and creatures help to balance the energy grid. Millions are being abused in unimaginable experiments or abused by evil people who harm and kill defenseless animals. they too are connected to the god consciousness, and I know that they have souls and evolve. What you do unto them, you do unto God. What abusive people do to animals does matter in the spiritual world, and there will be karma to pay.

During my childhood, we lived next to a row of large cottonwood trees, at least one hundred years old. I often climbed one and fantasized I could fly like a bird. I hid in the tree to escape my troubled home life. I felt safe within the embrace of the tree's huge branches, away from the harshness of life. I felt the tree's life and energy and sensed its soul.

Ancient people also believed trees had souls and treated them as animate beings that were to be respected and honored. In stories handed down by the Norse, the tree of the universe called *Yggdrasil*, symbolized all life. The Norse tree of life was a large ash tree, which connects the nine worlds and is the center of the cosmos.

The Cherokees, Lakota, and other American Indian tribes considered trees holy and sacred. They preferred to use trees that had already fallen instead of cutting down living trees. If a tree had to be cut, the people asked for permission from the tree, and gifts were offered for its life. They honored all life, including the animals they killed for food.

Trees are believed to serve as doorways to other worlds for shaman. The tree, in its wisdom, allows the shaman to transition to other worlds and realities. Certain tribes in California used tree stumps to embark on their sacred journeys. The Aboriginal Arunta of Australia use hollow trees to take spiritual journeys and the indigenous tribes of the Amazon follow the roots of the tree into the underworlds.

The remarkable thing about trees is that a single tree produces approximately 260 pounds of oxygen per year. Two mature trees supply enough oxygen annually to support a family of four! One tree can absorb as much carbon in a year as a car produces while driving 26,000 miles. It's as if trees were tailor-made for humans and all life to exist and thrive on Earth, and that's a miracle.

In 1997, a young environmentalist named Julia Butterfly Hill climbed a giant 200-foot California redwood in December and stayed there for 738 days to save the tree, dubbed *Luna*, from loggers ready to cut down the thousand-year-old tree. On December 18, 1999, Julia Butterfly Hill's feet touched the ground for the first time in over two years, as she descended from *Luna*, in Humboldt County, California.

Hill believed she would be there for a two-to-three week-long "tree-sit." The action was meant to stop Pacific Lumber, a division of the Maxxam Corporation, from the environmentally destructive process of clear-cutting the ancient redwood and the trees near it. The area immediately next to Luna had already been stripped and, because of that action, many believed there was nothing left to hold the soil to the mountain, a huge part of the hill from sliding into the town of Stafford.

Described in her book, *The Legacy of Luna*, Julia Hill wrote how she lived on a makeshift platform eighteen stories off the ground, enduring torrential storms, harassment from angry loggers, extreme cold, El-Nino storms, hurricane-force winds, helicopter harassment, and a ten-day siege by company security guards. But in her loneliness and doubt, she prayed to the Universal Spirit, to *Luna,* and heard the tree's voice speak to hear, teaching her to let go and to go with the flow.

Celebrities like Joan Baez, Bonnie Raitt, and Woody Harrelson visited the tree and Julia. Today, Hill continues her environmental activism. Sadly, only 3% of America's majestic ancient redwood forests remain. Now an even more disturbing problem has emerged as poachers enter California's national parks to removed large portions of the redwoods. In Northern California, redwood trees are being poached like the lawlessness taking place in the Amazon jungle. Thieves are cutting massive chunks from the base of the ancient trees, which are the tallest on Earth and are up to 2,000 years old. While state officials say the damage is far from any Amazonian deforestation, they do rank the desecration alongside elephant tusk poaching.

Although the trees can live when cut into, an open wound can cause pests and diseases to enter the trees and kill them, and it also becomes destabilized in large windstorms. These giants and all trees provide oxygen and remove pollutants in Earth's air and now they are being destroyed at an alarming rate. Insanity!

Grandmother Agnes Baker Pilgrim of Oregon says, "Life is very precious. Every blade of grass is our relative. Everyone one-legged—the Tree People—needs our voice. The animal kingdom and the swimmers in the water need our voice. They are crying out for help."

Grandmother Agnes also explained in *Grandmothers Counsel the World*, that in a single tree, there are four or five ecosystems, yet on the highways around the world, mighty trees are chained together onto log trucks, ancient giants heading for chipping mills, many to be shipped to Japan, where they are transformed into cardboard boxes to hold stereos, televisions, and other electronic equipment for eager consumers.

Grandmother Agnes has noted the harm clear-cut logging has done when the trees are no longer there to hold the moisture in the soil for the little shoots to grow. The elders of her community believe that if you take the trees off the top of the mountains, you change the climate because the ancient trees are the ones that call the wind and the rain. "Wind patterns are being destroyed; things that used to grow to hold the ground are being pulled up. Paving has caused erosion all over the lands."

In 1994 I attended a pow-wow ceremony in Kamiah, Idaho with the Nez Perce tribe, a gracious and kind people. One of the elders explained to me how clear-cutting of their sacred mountains had changed the weather in that region. Now they receive less rainfall each year.

Through my travels, I discovered that children are seldom taught how to respect nature. Although I did not witness the event at a local park, several trees had been stripped of their bark, perhaps by teens or children. Hopefully, these children didn't realize the damage they had inflicted on the tree by removing its protective skin. When trees lose their bark there are susceptible to insects, disease, and the elements. I pray that parents and schoolteachers will teach their children how valuable trees are to the world and our very survival. But teachers today, not all, seem to be too focused on teaching equity and racism with CTR (Critical Race Theory).

Today valuable trees found in rainforests throughout the world are being clear cut for planting crops and making room for a growing population. During my first visit to Belize in Central America, I was moved to tears where huge areas of forests were being cut and burned to plant orange groves and bananas crops. Environmentalists claim they are killing the natural habitats of indigenous animals and contributing to climate change. Clearcutting has caused the loss of topsoil. A study from the University of Oregon found that in certain zones, clear-cut areas, had nearly three times the amount of erosion and slides. Demand for wood and arable land through clear-cutting has led to the loss of over half of the world's rainforests.

The world's rainforests could completely vanish in a hundred years at the current rate of deforestation. Between June 2000 and June 2008 more than 150 000 square kilometers of rainforest were cleared in the Brazilian Amazon. As the rainforests of the world disappear so do thousands of plants that have medicinal and healing powers. According to a recent estimate, over 5,000 different species of medicinal herbs and plants exist at present in rainforests worldwide. These plants have been used by healers, shamans, and other tribal people for thousands of years, but could now vanish if we don't take action to save them.

My mentor, Western Shoshone spiritual leader Corbin Harney said it best, "We have to come back to the Native way of life. The Native way is to pray for everything, to take care of everything. We see what's taking place: the animal life has begun to show us, the tree life is showing us, and the water is even telling us, but we're not paying attention to it.

"People today don't realize that what's out there—all the things growing on the land—needs to have our prayers. These things are here on the Earth with us. We're part of their life too, and together this is how we are to survive over the long term."

In the PBS documentary, *What Plants Talk About,* experimental plant ecologist Dr. J.C. Cahill made some astonishing information about plants and how they eavesdrop on each other, talk to their allies, call on insect mercenaries and nurture their young. We think of plants as none-thinking, none-hearing, none-seeing, yet they can find food, communicate with each other, and even wage war. If a plant is injured or under attack by insects, animals, or even humans, it puts out a chemical S.O.S. Like all of Earth's nature, life has evolved for survival. Even without eyes, a brain, ears, plants do communicate through chemicals they release—it's just that modern humans have forgotten how complex and evolved they truly are.

It has been documented those plants are capable of "intent" and emotional response. They respond to the world around them, to bees, to insects, to sunlight and darkness, to wind, to drought and rains. Have you ever noticed that a dandelion, a profuse weed, can grow anywhere? In the wild, the dandelion grows to several feet high, yet when it grows in your yard it stays only high enough to escape the lethal blades of your lawn mower. Dandelions are very clever and have adapted well.

One of the first scientists to describe plants as having consciousness was a Viennese biologist named Raoul Francé. He stated that plants were capable of astonishing perception and even communication. He further felt that plants reacted to abuse and appeared thankful for kindness. Scientists in the early twentieth century ignored Francé's findings, but in the 1960s his findings were confirmed by researchers who proved that plants do possess the ability to communicate with humans.

Another scientist to understand the complexity of plants was Luther Burbank (1849-1926), who was well-known for plant cross-pollination and selective breeding. He stated that "the secret of improved plant breeding is love." One of his extraordinary experiments was the development of the spineless cactus, which was used for feeding livestock. Burbank said he spoke gently to the cacti, thereby letting them know they would not need their thorns. By creating an environment of love and trust, he was able to eventually breed a new thornless variety. (I wonder if the plant was truly happy with that outcome!).

In 1939, a man named Semyon Kirlian accidentally discovered that if an object on a photographic plate was connected to a high-voltage source, an image appeared on the photographic plate. Kirlian photography, although the study of which can be traced back to the late 1700s, was officially invented in 1939 by Semyon Davidovitch Kirlian. The Kirlian photographic process revealed visible "auras" around the objects photographed. These photographs became the subject of great skepticism and controversy over the years.

The process involved a sheet of photographic film placed on top of a metal plate. The object to be photographed was then placed on top of the film. To create the initial exposure, a high voltage current was then applied to the metal plate. The electrical coronal discharge between the object and the metal plate was captured on film, producing a glowing aura around the silhouetted object as a result of developing the film.

Kirlian and his wife Valentina didn't make their discovery known until 1958, but it took until 1970 for the phenomenon to become widely known. During this time, Kirlian photography expanded into photographs of human subjects, animals, and just about anything else.

Results of scientific experiments published in 1976 involving Kirlian photography of living tissue (human fingertips) showed that most of the variations in corona discharge streamer length, density, curvature, and color can be accounted for by the moisture content on the surface of and within the living tissue.

In the early 1970s, I had the good fortune of meeting Dr. Thelma Moss, a psychology professor at UCLA's

Neuropsychiatric Institute (NPI), later renamed the Semel Institute, through a mutual friend. Dr. Moss and the NPI had a laboratory dedicated to parapsychology research and staffed mostly with volunteers. I had hoped to be one of her volunteers, but unfortunately, distance and work prevented me from getting involved. Eventually, the lab was shut down by the university. Toward the end of her tenure at UCLA, Dr. Moss became interested in Kirlian photography.

I deeply regret not accepting Dr. Moss's offer to volunteer at the lab and learn more about Kirlian photography and the human aura from this amazing woman. Dr. Moss also explored a wide range of specific subjects in parapsychology such as hypnosis, ghosts, levitation, and alternative medicine.

Places like England, Ireland, and Scotland have long been known for their legends and folklore of fairies, elves, devas, and elementals; nature's spirits that dwell in the forests. They are the unseen intelligent beings who inhabit the four elements (Air, Earth, Fire, and Water), which they were made. Theosophists Charles Webster Leadbeater and Alice A. Bailey suggested that devas represent a separate evolution from humanity. The concept of devas as nature spirits derives from the writings of Theosophist Geoffrey Hodson. Theosophists believe there are numerous different types of devas with a population in the millions performing different functions on Earth to help the ecology function better. It is asserted they can be observed by those whose third eyes have been activated.

In addition, it is believed by Theosophists that there are millions of devas living inside the Sun, the indwelling solar deity which Theosophists call the "Solar Logos"—these devas are called solar angels, or sometimes solar devas or solar spirits. It is believed they visit Earth and can be observed, like other devas, by humans when the third eye has been activated. Theosophists believe that there are also devas living inside all the other stars besides the sun and they are called stellar angels.

Water Spirits
Of all the planets in our Solar System, Earth stands out as the only unique "blue planet." When viewed from outer space, Earth is a vivid blue marble, where water covers 70.9 percent of our planet's surface. No other planet in the entire solar system has an ocean and ecology like Earth.

Due to climate change, great droughts in the last twenty-plus years had dried up lakes throughout the world. Pure drinking water is vanishing at an unprecedented rate.

Less than 5 percent of that water is fresh, and much of it is locked up in ice sheets or deep within the ground. Today, our oceans, rivers, lakes, and streams are polluted by sewage, industrial waste, pesticides, oil, and radiation from the Fukushima nuclear plant in Japan.

When I was growing up the thought of paying for a bottle of filtered drinking water would have been a ludicrous thought, yet here we are in the twenty-first century drinking purified water from plastic bottles. With well over 7.2 billion humans on the planet, and growing, our natural resources are vanishing at an unprecedented rate. At the rate that we are consuming water plus the severe drought affecting many areas of the world, we have a perfect storm for global water wars.

Historian David Soll wrote in his book, *Empire Water*, "Clean water is no longer a free gift of nature. It is a shared resource that can be preserved only through judicious investments and active engagement." Water is a living entity with consciousness. We can no longer look at water in the same over-abundant way and think it will flourish from our neglect. We must view it as a sacred living, breathing entity like our ancestors did or it will perish, and so will we.

Water is an amazing substance that can transform into many forms, ice, steam, snow, and a fluid state. Water is the most life-sustaining gift of Mother Earth, her lifeblood. Without water, most living inhabitants on this planet would not exist. Water flows outside us and within us, and it cleanses, and it heals everything. Life grows from it and flourishes.

The element of water teaches us that it has great power to cut down the tallest mountains and create the deepest canyons and should be respected for its immense strength. Archaeologists have recently discovered ancient cities that vanished beneath the oceans thousands of years ago, destroyed by a deluge of water.

Water can be soft, cold, hot, and healing but is always transmutable and ever-changing like human emotions. Water teaches us to be flexible and gentle, fierce and powerful and at the end of our life journey, we too flow into the great ocean of unknown. Water shapes the land with rivers, lakes, glaciers, mountains, and canyons. Water is the home of countless organisms that contribute to the life cycle of planet Earth. It is one giant symbiotic organism.

New research at the Aerospace Institute of the University of Stuttgart in Germany supports the theory that water has memory. Experiments revealed that each droplet of water from the same source has a different face. Each unique. They wondered if water has an "imprint" of energies to which it had been exposed. The theory was first proposed by the late French immunologist Dr. Jacques Benveniste in a controversial article published in 1988 in *Nature* as a way of explaining how homeopathy works.

If Benveniste is right, just think what that might mean to the world. More than 70 percent of our planet is covered in water and the human body is made up of 60 percent water; the brain, 70 percent; the lungs, nearly 90 percent. Our energies might be traveling out of our brains and bodies and into those of other living beings of all kinds through imprints on this magical substance. Think of how rivers and lakes carry an infinitesimal amount of information and data, and when we drink from them, we are infused with the information at a cellular level. So, oceans and rivers and rains might be transporting all manner of information throughout the world—both positive and negative.

The First Nations peoples of North America have a special relationship with water, built on their subsistence ways of life that extend back thousands of years. Their traditional activities depend on water for transportation, drinking, cleaning, purification, and providing habitat for the plants and animals they gather as medicines and foods. Their ability to access good water shapes these traditional activities and their relationships with their surroundings. As Indigenous peoples, First Nations recognized the sacredness of their water, the interconnectedness of all life, and the importance of protecting their water from pollution, drought, and waste.

Water is the giver of all life and without clean water, all life on Earth would perish.

Indigenous people throughout the world have always claimed a special relationship with nature. Many shaman and medicine men have called upon the water spirits to bring rain to drought areas. Remarkably their prayers and ceremonies are heard, and rain is produced. It is said the term "Rain Dance" came into being during the days of Native American relocation by the U.S. government which banned certain religious ceremonies like the Ghost Dance or Sun Dance. The tribes in suppressed areas were forbidden to perform the Sun Dance, so they called it their "Rain Dance." Today the rain dance has been passed down through oral tradition, and many American Indians keep these rituals alive today.

Aboriginal people in the traditional communities of the far north of the Northern Territory of Australia still practice their ancient ceremonies and rituals. These remain of crucial importance to their lives and involve the whole community. Often these ceremonies are strongly associated with death, or, more precisely, for the souls of people who have departed from this life and joined the "Dreaming," the timeless continuum of past, present, and future. Sacred Dreaming is where mythological ancestral beings traveled and caused the natural features of the country to come into being by their actions.

In Numbulwar, an aboriginal tribe on the eastern shore of the Gulf of Carpentaria has a ceremony called "Ngarrag." Actors begin first and then the Yirritja men are painted with designs representing their "Dreaming" or clan association. There are many different rituals, some taking place on secret ceremonial grounds, where they assume the spirit beings of the planet. The ceremony ends in the ritual of bathing where the entire clan goes to the beach and immerses themselves, dancing in the sea and washing off the ochre and clay that was painted on them earlier in the ceremony. Dreamtime beings of the mythical past leave them in their songs and painted designs on their bodies behind and re-emerge from the water as people again.

Water creates our weather. Water evaporates as vapor from oceans, lakes, and rivers; is transpired from plants; condenses in the air and falls as precipitation; and then moves over and through the ground into water bodies, where the cycle begins again. Mother Nature is a perfect organism.

Moving water found in ocean waves, waterfalls, rivers, release negatively charged ions in the atmosphere. Negative and positive ions refer to electrical charge plus or minus. Negative electrical charges have good effects on humans, while positive-charged ions have bad effects on our health.

The word ion is derived from the Greek word meaning, "to go" or "to move." An ion is an atom or molecule in which the total number of electrons is not equal to the total number of protons, giving the atom a net positive or negative electrical charge. Ions can be produced in nature and by chemical means. An atom is electrically neutral when the number of electrons surrounding the nucleus (or nuclei) is equal to the atomic number. It becomes a positive ion if one or more electrons is missing, or it becomes a negative ion if it has one more extra electron.

For eons, prophets, sages, and wisdom keepers have sought higher spiritual experiences and consciousness on mountains or near waterfalls or oceans. This is no accident—negative ions can be found in the air near waterfalls, mountains, beaches, and forests. These are among those places where ionization levels are the highest in nature.

The Greek physician Hippocrates noted 2,300 years ago that his patients benefited from taking long walks near the sea or in the mountains. Even baptism in "living water" marks the beginning of Christianity as written in the Bible when John the Baptist was baptized by Jesus in the Jordan River.

Jesus was said to have harnessed stormy seas by calming water and walking upon it. The miracle described how Jesus sent his disciples by ship to the other side of the Sea of Galilee while he remained behind to pray. As night fell a windstorm created huge waves for the ship. Amid the storm, the disciples saw Jesus walking on the sea toward them. Frightened, they thought they were seeing a spirit when Jesus told them not to be afraid. Jesus then entered the ship and calmed the storm, and they arrived safely onshore. According to a detailed account found only in Matthew, Peter could also "walk on water," but he became afraid and began to sink, but Jesus rescued him. Was this a literal story or one that was used to teach a lesson of faith or what humans can accomplish if they believe in their power? Perhaps both.

It is believed that Michel de Nostre-Dame—Nostradamus, an astrologer and a physician from the sixteenth century, used water and astrology to divine the past, present, and future. It is believed he used a bowl of water to see into the future. He used a tripod to hold the bowl then touched the tripod with the wand, dipped the wand in the water and then touched the hem of his robe. He then looked deep into the water and viewed the future. Many believed that Nostradamus used a form of self-hypnosis or meditation. Some followers of Nostradamus even believe he foretold events into the twentieth and twenty-first centuries in the year 1555 that included predictions of Hitler, World War I and II, and even John F. Kennedy's assassination written in his book, *The Centuries.*

Did Nostradamus remote view by concentrating on the bowl of water? Perhaps he understood the power of water to project an image of the future when one meditates on a question. The most common media for scrying or viewing the future was the use of a reflective, translucent, or luminescent substance such as crystals, stones, glass, mirrors, water, fire, or smoke.

Waterfalls have the highest concentration of negative ions, but negative ions can be found in mountains, rapid moving water such as rivers and oceans, and dense vegetation such as forests or rain forests.

While living in Los Angeles, California for twenty-five years, I made an interesting observation during dry, hot Santa Ana winds and how the winds affect people. They'd become irritable and ill-tempered. The dry wind creates positive ions that can cause people to experience headaches, depression, and an inability to concentrate. Similar winds in the United States known as Chinooks created the same phenomena in humans. In other places around the world, the dry winds are known as Sirocco, Zonda, Khamsin, and Mistral. In France, during the Mistral winds, more crimes are committed similar to the full moon phenomena.

Have you noticed how you feel before a major electrical storm where positive ions dance around the sky and ground? The ions in a cloud behave in the same way as the ions in a waterfall. The kinetic energy in the turbulent airstrips off the electrons, leaving positive-charged ions. These free electrons are picked up by other atoms and molecules to create the negative-charged ions. The clouds are negatively charged, and the Earth's surface becomes positively charged creating lightning. So, if you feel irritable and out of sorts, blame those positive-charged ions.

Lightning ionizes the air, providing more free ions after the lightning strikes. American Indians have reported many cases of visions connected during thunder and lightning storms. I've also discovered that during electrical storms I experience increased psychic abilities and increased energy. Is it any wonder that indigenous people, shamans, and holy people, throughout the world, understood the significance of ions and sought the mountains, waterfalls, oceans, and forests for visions, spiritual enlightenment, and clarity of thought?

Once the storm is underway and rain begins to fall, you will feel much better, even restful, and at peace from the negative-charged ions.

In Jerusalem, researchers discovered that some people have sensitivity to barometric pressure. Their levels of serotonin in the brain increased just before and during desert wind conditions due to the positive ions. However, the serotonin dropped when these people were placed in negative-ionized rooms. Research conducted in France, Germany, Italy, and especially Russia found significant health benefits of health spas if they were situated near waterfalls. In Russia, such places are called "electrical resorts." In Japan, waterfalls are considered powerful *kami*, where divine spirits reside.

Japanese author and entrepreneur Dr. Masara Emoto (1943-2014) was an internationally renowned researcher who gained worldwide acclaim by demonstrating how water is deeply connected to our individual and collective consciousness.

Emoto's ideas first appeared in the popular documentary, *What the Bleep Do We Know!?*. Although Emoto's work was widely considered pseudoscience that directly violates basic physics, his remarkable photographs of ice crystals proved something wonderous was at work. His photographic work of water crystals was published in his book, *Message from Water, Vol. I, II, and III,* and sold over one million copies internationally in twenty-two languages. Emoto's other book, *The Hidden Messages in Water,* sold over 500,000 print copies.

Through the 1990's, Dr. Emoto performed a series of experiments observing the physical effect of words, prayers, music, and environment on the crystalline structure of water. Emoto hired photographers to take pictures of water after being exposed to the different variables including frozen water so that they would form crystalline structures. The results were nothing short of extraordinary.

The experiments possibly proved that our thoughts have a major impact on our environment. That concept is relatively easy to grasp, but this extremely tangible evidence proved amazing. If our words and thoughts have this effect on water crystals, just think what consciousness *en masse* could produce? Our thoughts coalesce into solid matter, and as Dr. Emoto discovered, human thought can transform water molecules.

Eventually, Emoto formed his non-profit organization, "International Water for Life," through which he dedicated his water research to achieving world peace.

There are incredible dynamics taking place in our oceans that began approximately 4.54 billion years ago. Scientists don't know how Earth arrived to be a water planet. Mars does contain polar ice and Jupiter's moon Ganymede is composed of approximately equal amounts of silicate rock and water ice, but nothing like Planet Earth. The most popular theory for Earth's water is that shortly after Earth formed, millions of asteroids and comets, saturated in water, slammed into our planet, releasing their water to form oceans, which sounds a bit preposterous to me. Still, there are mysteries about the formation of our planet's oceans, lakes, and rivers.

Whenever I swim in a river, lake, or ocean, I always talk to the water spirits and give thanks for their gift of life. On several occasions, my life was saved by honoring the water spirits while rafting and scuba diving.

As Corbin Harney said, "There is a sickness among us today, and it is very sad to see these things; the earth, air, and water are becoming more and more contaminated. We're going to have to put our thoughts together to save our planet here. We only have One Water...One Air...One Mother Earth.

"Our Indian belief is, we are Natives of the land, and so we have to be with it. But nowadays we haven't been doing what we've been told to do, to be with the land. We have to take care of the living things here, all the plants, all the animal life. When we take the life of an animal, we have to tell it why we're taking its life. It has to know the reason. Then we give the animal a blessing and then we also give something back of whatever we're taking.

"We can't just go out and harvest whatever we want to. We have to talk to each living thing and bless it and say the reason why we're taking its life—the plant, the animal, the birdlife, whatever. If they were to take our life, we'd want to understand why they were taking it. These are our strong beliefs."

Corbin believed, like his ancestors before him, that water and all life on Earth is a living entity, and we must reconnect with our Mother Earth through prayers, ceremonies, and talking to everything again.

Animal Spirits

Indigenous cultures speak of the mystery and communication between humans and Mother Nature's creatures. Animals are psychic and can predict extreme weather and sense earthquakes and other disasters long before they happen. Stories abound of dogs and cats that can predict earthquakes, predict their owner's death and forewarn humans of a disaster. They have even been known to travel great distances to find their owner.

I've had many pets since childhood—cats, dogs, horses, a rabbit, a turtle, and two birds, an owl and robin I nursed back to health. Each pet had a unique personality and intelligence. There were even times when I felt a telepathic link with them. I know in my heart that animals have souls and when they die, they join us on the Other Side. They even reincarnate and join us on great adventures lifetime after lifetime. I've always believed that everything is evolving and growing spiritually, including all life forms visible and invisible.

Buddhists have always regarded animals as sentient beings. Animals possess Buddha-nature and have the potential for enlightenment like all consciousness. Buddhists believe in rebirth, and that any human could be reborn as an animal, and any animal could be reborn as a human. They also take the concept a bit further and believe that sentient beings currently residing in the animal realm have been our mothers, brothers, sisters, fathers, children, and friends in past lives.

Animals were given to us on Mother Earth as companions and teachers, even those we eat. If animals killed for food were taken with love and respect, then the animal spirit would gladly give up its physical body. But presently, we do not honor the animals we eat; instead, they are treated as if they were not alive, as if they don't feel pain and have intellect. A great many animals on this planet are abused and with it comes a great karmic lesson. Perhaps if we all held all living creatures in reverence like Buddhist monks, life on this planet would have evolved much faster. Buddhist monks even try to avoid killing insects, and if they do happen to step on a bug, they pray for its soul.

Ed McGaa "Eagle Man" said, "If I take a four-legged or catch a finned, I tell it that I am taking it to provide and I thank it. Many finned I put back into the water and let them go." It is this relationship with all living things that we must honor again.

There are stories animals were brought here from other planets where they were evolved sentient beings. They were biogenetically engineered to be our companions and to seed Earth. In ancient Egypt, the cat, both small and large, were considered deities because they held great information and monitored their human family. Is it any wonder that lions and cats cover the walls of ancient temples? The ancients' believed cats were transmitters to extraterrestrial species.

After years of owning several wonderful cats, I've seen how telepathic they can be. Dogs are just as intuitive. Isn't it ironic how our pets know what time we'll arrive home from work? Our cat Comet saved my husband and me late one night. Comet appeared upset, going in and out of his cat door from the living room to the garage. That wasn't like him. My husband finally got up to see what the commotion was all about and made a shocking discovery in our garage—gasoline had leaked from our VW camper bus and was moving toward the gas heater. If Comet hadn't persisted, we would have had a disastrous fire.

Cats see ghosts and spirits. One night Comet was in the hallway of our house with his fur on end, hissing and staring up at a photograph of my departed sister Kathy in the hallway. I know Kathy was there in spirit. There had been other confirmations of her presence during that time, and I told him to calm down. He seemed fine after that.

According to the ancients, animals exist in two realities—our 3-D world and the spirit world, and access both worlds all day and night. Cats live in two worlds all the time and see spirits and ghosts. At this time, animals are mirroring the pain humans are feeling psychologically, spiritually, and physically. That's why our pets have cancers, obesity, and diabetes. They mirror what we need to learn about ourselves. When we learn what we do to ourselves, we do to the planet and all life, and then we will be ready to sit in council with advanced beings of higher planes. We will finally comprehend how the God force exists in all things. We will learn that as humans we aren't the only intelligent species or the most evolved.

Elephants grieve for the death of their own, dogs and cats have been known to grieve for their owners and other animals. Perhaps the most enticing quality of elephants is their undeniable similarity to humans: they have close bonds they form with family members; they communicate with each other, they have a long-life span, they care for and protect their young, they have great intelligence, and they have emotions—many of the same emotions as people do. Elephants are capable of sadness, joy, love, jealousy, fury, grief, compassion, and distress. Moreover, we see these same attributes in our pets.

When an elephant dies, the herd will take great care in the burial. Cows walk to and fro in search of leaves and twigs to cover the body of their deceased in an act of dignity for their dead. When a herd encounters the skeleton of a dead elephant, they have shown a great fascination for the skeleton as the cows caress the bones. The cows then take the bones and scatter them, hiding them under bushes in the surrounding area. Even years later, elephants have been observed revisiting the place where one of their family members died. They will remain there for days at a time, in mourning.

There are stories of whales and dolphins guiding ships and dolphins saving humans adrift in the ocean. Sadly, a great number of the cetaceans are taken from their families and mothers and put into small tanks for human entertainment. Whales and dolphins are part of a huge social group of sea creatures, in which individuals are dependent upon each other. Remove them from both these aspects of their lives, and the claustrophobic effects upon them can become catastrophic. Depression, physical illness, and aberrant behavior have all been revealed in the 2013 documentary *Blackfish*. The documentary focused on Tilikum, an orca held by SeaWorld, and the controversy over the captive killer whale, which ended in the death of three people. Taking these giants of the water from their mothers and placing them in small pools to perform tricks for large crowds is inhuman and abusive.

In addition, those orcas taken into captivity from the wild are not the only ones that suffer. The pods that are left behind may depend upon them for many social reasons, and vital bonds necessary for orca survival can be broken as key members are taken from family groups. Orcas and dolphins taken from their pods can never be reintroduced to the wild again. They become outcasts and can never rejoin a pod again. The movie, *Free Willy*, was not based on fact!

Animals of the world do not belong in cages for human entertainment. They need to be respected and honored and left to enjoy their freedom. Whenever humans interfere with nature, introduce a new species to nature, whether animals or plants, the consequences are usually disastrous. Nature has its own perfect balance.

Animal Sixth Sense

Witnesses reported that shortly before the 9.3 megathrust earthquake hit Indonesia on December 26, 2004, animals such as elephants and monkeys rushed for higher ground, and cattle, dogs, and domestic animals showed anxiety. Surprisingly, few dead animals were recovered after the tsunami hit coastal areas, but 230,000 human lives were lost that day.

Whether animals have a sixth sense or just feel unusual vibrations or changes in air pressure coming from one direction is debatable among researchers. If a herd of animals is seen fleeing before an earthquake, all that is needed is for one or two of them to skittishly sense danger. When you think about it, we shouldn't be surprised by animal sixth sense. Feral animals have excellent senses of smell, sight, hearing, and even the ability to sense minute vibrations because they've evolved those senses to survive. Many species perceive and use electromagnetic fields to navigate or find prey that is imperceptible to humans.

A few years ago, I watched the award-winning documentary *The Animal Communicator,* about Anna Breytenbach, a South African-based professional animal communicator who received advanced training through the Assisi International Animal Institute in California, USA. Born and raised in Cape Town, South Africa, she holds a degree in Psychology, Economics, and Marketing from the University of Cape Town. Anna lives out her passion for wildlife and conservation by volunteering at various rehabilitation and educational centers.

Anna has dedicated her life to what she calls "interspecies communication." In the documentary, Anna was asked to help with a black leopard living at South Africa's Jukani Wildlife Sanctuary. The Olsens, the young couple who owned the Jukani Wildlife Sanctuary, had rescued a vicious, snarling black leopard from Europe named Diablo. They had other wild cats in their care and never had any problem with them until Diablo came to their sanctuary. After six months in the sanctuary, Diablo never left his night shelter. He hissed and snarled, and had even bitten Mr. Olsen's hand once, landing him in the hospital for a week. He and his wife didn't want to get rid of Diablo, but they didn't know what to do with him.

Anna was then called in to help without any prior knowledge of the cat. What happened next was nothing short of miraculous. As soon as Anna came near the angry leopard, he instantly calmed down and let her knell beside his cage. As the big cat and Anna stared into each other eyes, she began to sense the leopard was awed by his new surroundings but still stressed by the treatment he received at his prior residence. She sensed the beautiful leopard had been abused and had become wary of humans.

Anna believed the leopard had both physical power and great wisdom and personality that commanded respect—but not in a needy way. After communicating with Diablo, it was established that he didn't understand that he was safe there, and free to roam, relax and be at ease. He told Anna that he didn't like the name, Diablo—that wasn't who he was. It brought forth negativity and darkness.

Diablo then asked Anna about the two young cubs that were at the zoo, something she had not been told about. Both Mr. and Mrs. Olsen were stunned by his information—they had not told Anna that Diablo had been with two small cub leopards at the zoo.

In the following days, Mr. and Mrs. Olsen changed Diablo's name to "Spirit" and shortly afterward, the great cat began to explore his new surroundings outside his night shelter. One day Mr. Olsen decided to talk to Spirit and told him he was safe there, that they would make no demands of him. He began telling Spirit how beautiful he was, and each time the big cat would reply in a low growl. This went on nineteen times!

Upon Anna's return to the sanctuary, Mr. Olsen explained the interaction he had with Spirit on that day. Anna explained the big cat was appreciative of his kind words and that surprised him. It made Spirit stop in his tracks. Spirit was replying "thank you" to Mr. Olsen's "beautiful" remarks.

Although a skeptic at first about animal communication, Mr. Olsen was overcome by emotion, filling him with awe he couldn't express in words. That's when he realized that he could also communicate with wild cats. He and his wife have since taken Anna's class on interspecies communication.

Learning to communicate with animals is to practice being present and fully aware with all senses—to be in a state of acceptance, love, trust, gentleness, and calm. It is a form of meditation where we quiet our minds to allow conversation with other creatures. Sometimes an animal or plant may not want to communicate, and this boundary should be respected. Their language is not our human language. It's a language older than words, transference of thought. Anna in her teachings of interspecies communication says this is our birthright. We all have this ability if learned. It's called intuition.

We are connected to animal spirits, the elementals, the rocks, the water, and the winged, finned, and four-legged creatures.

In the realm of multidimensionality and merging, animals are adepts. Animals move through dimensions. Have you ever seen an animal or a bird one minute, and then the next second it vanished? My husband and I experienced what we called "the white flash," a spirit or something unknown that moved so quickly we couldn't identify in the country club we lived at in Henderson, Nevada. We both witnessed the "white flash" twice, and I sensed it was ancient indigenous people who had lived in the area hundreds of years ago.

Animals are very concerned with the quality of life—much more so than humans are. When the quality of life is in question, animals automatically migrate toward a more sustaining reality. They remove themselves into other domains of existence, for they are programmed to survive.

Animals are intelligent and flexible and have many more adventures than humans do. Animals don't need to build shopping malls, graveyards, watch television and movies, and distract themselves with superficial forms of entertainment. Do you think animals ever get bored? Do you think animals ever wonder what to do next? They have many, many adventures that you are not quite capable of understanding, though you will one day.

Insects and frogs, for example, open dimensional avenues with their sounds. Others may travel on sound. Everything dreams, journeying into many realities. You can best relate to the concept of dreaming knowing that, when you sleep, you go into another world that does exist. Everything exists because it is connected, whether memory is open or not. Beetles, earthworms, and frogs know they go from one reality to another. They go into other worlds, yet they are right here in this world.

Insects work with us in a way we cannot conceive at this time. You think they just accidentally land or crawl on you when in actuality they are checking out your electromagnetic frequency. You do not look like yourself to insects. You are a force field, and certain parts of you are very attractive to insects because of the pheromones you give off.

Many forms of life will come to awareness and existence. You will want to capture these forms of life and put them in a zoo. To them, you are in the zoo, like a prison, locked behind bars. They want to assist you and bring you back to interspecies communication. They are waiting to see if you can relate to particular animals or species. As you demonstrate your acknowledgment of intelligence in all forms of life, you begin to qualify as an ambassador or diplomatic representative of these various species. Life will become very strange indeed.

When a frog makes a croaking sound, it creates an opening to other dimensions for the animal kingdom—for insects in particular, but many members of the animal kingdom. Frogs and insects keep frequency and have certain abilities. Frogs, when they croak in the stillness of the day or night, create a harmonic and a spinning momentum. Surrounding energies can move into this sound and experience what it is like to be in other forms of life quite easily.

All animals are much more in tune with multiple realities than humans are, and they can teach you about these realities. Some people can merge with animals and explore the animal kingdom to discover what it is like to be in the Living Library. Many very intelligent forms of life can manifest themselves by merging with the animal and plant kingdoms.

You see, all life plays a major part in holding the balance of Mother Earth when they tone—the sounds they make. They help hold Earth's grid together.

In this way, animals and insects can peek into your reality. Now, these many intelligent forms of life want to merge with humans. As we prepare ourselves to merge with other forms of sentient existence, you will be able to bring peace to Mother Earth. You will be able to bring a magnificent new upliftment, a new way of being, a new prayer, and a new reverence. It will seem as if it is coming out of you, and yet you will know that it is more than you. Understand that there is great intelligence in all life forms, and the experience of all life is waiting for you.

Open your emotional selves and employ the vital force of love as the key to your own spiritual evolution. Realize that all life is evolving in the Universe, and animals have souls. Those who harm or abuse animals think their actions won't count in the spiritual scheme of things, but they are wrong. Every word, every action, every thought is recorded in the Akashic records and there is retribution.

When you drive, be sure to put up invisible barriers by asking your Spirit Guides to allow you to drive safely and never hit or injure an animal. Whenever I drive long distances, I always say a prayer for protection, and it works!

Through the years, I've been blessed with special pets—horses, dogs, cats, a rabbit, and a bird, and I always believed that they should be treated the way that I'd want to be treated—with love, compassion, and kindness. I've never viewed them as just animals, but as evolving souls, part of the God-consciousness.

Betty Andreasson Luca and Bob Luca have been abducted by aliens through the years. In the book, *The Watchers II*, by Raymond Fowler, Bob under hypnosis was told this by the aliens about animals. "Man will be very surprised to find where animals fit in. All that is done is recorded, (Akashic Records), and many foolish people think the harm they've done to animals will not count. It will! All that the Creator's made is not to be taken lightly. And the most lowly to the most magnificent, much is to be learned."

When Bob was asked if evil will be wiped away and about human spirituality, he said, "There will come a time when evil will be wiped away. That time is not close at hand. When that time comes, our growth will not cease. Rather, we will advance into further planes of existence. Right now, that type of society that you speak of is not possible because the people of this plane as a whole are not very advanced spiritually. Technology is advancing. Spirituality, unfortunately, is not keeping pace."

I've always known that our pets have souls, reincarnate and follow us through each lifetime. I have been given proof that animals live on in the spiritual realm.

My sister loved animals and had horses, cats, dogs, and a parrot through the years. And that hasn't changed since her passing. I imagine Kathy with a menagerie of spirit animals around her, caring for them and helping them ease over to the Other Side.

Cats are also incredibly psychic. A few years ago, there was a cat in the news who lived in a senior home care center. That cat always warned whenever one of the senior citizens was going to die by jumping up in its lap.

My cousin Mary is a cat lady who has owned many cats through the years. Several have passed through the years, but they visit her as dancing orbs of light in her bedroom. She has several videos from her bedroom camcorder of orbs flying in every direction. One video displays her living cat walking through the bedroom as the orbs follow it into the bathroom (see photo below).

In 2007, my husband and I purchased a four-month-old black and white Havanese puppy. We named him Oreo because of his black and white coloring and white streak in the middle of his head between two black ears. He was smart, learned tricks instantly, and learned countless words during his time with us 24 hours, seven days a week. We called him our "Velcro dog" because he followed me everywhere, and often cried if I went shopping or was gone for over an hour.

In 2016, I had several life-threatening surgeries, and Oreo was upset that I had been in the hospital for several days. My husband had placed some pajamas on a kitchen chair to take to the hospital and Oreo pulled them off the chair and slept on them. He hated being left alone for more than an hour and often howled like a wolf.

In 2020, we learned he had an enlarged heart causing a heart murmur, but he was still doing well for his advanced age. His cough became worse, and our veterinarian prescribed several medications that helped a little. By Christmas 2021, we knew that it was time to put him down. We discovered a local veterinarian who would euthanize Oreo at our home in a loving atmosphere. She arrived at our home on January 4, 2022, at noon. Oreo had been depressed and lethargic that morning and didn't eat much. It was as if he knew intuitively it was his time to die probably because my departed sister had prepared him for the crossover.

I asked my spirit sister Kathy to guide him over to the other side and hoped she had heard me. On New Year's Day, inexplicable things began to happen. Doors shut by themselves—the one to our laundry room and our bedroom. I sensed Kathy had heard my request and was proofing she had arrived.

The day before Oreo was to be put down, he had a burst of energy as if he was a puppy again—happy and wagging his tail. Humans rally the same way before dying. Two days before, doors began to shut by themselves. Both the laundry room door and our master bedroom door shut. Early morning on the day Oreo was going to be euthanized, he ended up on the bedroom side and had a look of surprise when the door shut on him by itself. Many times, I sensed he had seen Kathy. Ten minutes before the vet arrived, the door to our bedroom shut again.

Oreo was placed on my lap and was like he was ready to go as I held him in our arms with my husband beside me until he passed peacefully. Kathy was there to help him transition. But that wasn't the end of Oreo. The door to our bedroom has closed many times since his passing. Recently, my husband and I had errands to run and had been gone from the house for nearly four hours. We returned to find the door closed, knowing Oreo was upset that we had been gone too long. He never liked leaving him alone for more than one hour.

January 28, 2022, Oreo closed our bedroom door. We had gone out in the morning to run some errands, and before leaving I notice the bedroom door was ajar as if he was pushing it. When we returned home around 11:20 am, the door was opened more. I spoke to Oreo and told him to push the door closed, and then I walked out of the room for a few seconds. When I returned the door was shut! Check out our spirit dog Oreo pushing our bedroom door closed on YouTube.

https://www.youtube.com/watch?v=prJ44EiAH_I
This activity continues almost daily.

Although my husband and I have shed many tears, and miss

his physical presence, we know he's still here with us in spirit. He was smart and we talked to him like a human for 15 years. I'm sure that had a lot to do with him staying with us. We feel blessed to have 15 years of his humorous antics, his sweetness, and his intelligence. If you feel that you have known your pet before, no doubt you have. They sojourn with us from lifetime to lifetime.

Our beloved dog Oreo

Losing a pet is heartbreaking because they are our four-legged children. Each pet has an individual personality. We'd never trade the experience of having a pet. Who could deny that our pets help us live fuller lives, bring us joy, unconditional love, and companionship? It's a chance for them and for us to grow and evolve. They never die, but go to the Other Side, like all life, and they are only a vibration away.

Even insects go to the other side. In many ways, the Other Side is a reflection of the living world. Insects don't have souls, but they do have consciousness, and evolve. I've held a bee when it fell asleep on a flower and warmed it up, and within minutes it flew away. Insects are intuitive and have evolved for millions of years. Like plants, they know if you are going to harm them.

If we are kind to our pets, we get an excellent grade in karma, and so do our pets. Just think of all the pets—horses, dogs, cats that have saved human lives and other pets. They get elevated for their good deeds too.

I urge any of you that see an animal being mistreated to report it. Dogs are left in cars on hot days and die, or they are left in the back of a pickup truck on a hot day causing their paws to be burned. Treat them like it was your child. They are!

All LIFE SHOULD ALWAYS BE HONORED, CHERISHED, AND RESPECTED.

*Dear Globalists, 'We the People' have reviewed your proposal
for 'The Great Reset, and regret to inform you that we will
have to decline at this time. Although we did find the free trial
of the 'New World Order' interesting, we have decided instead
to go with 'The Great Awakening.'* Sincerely, The Human Race

AFTERWORD

THE GREAT AWAKENING

Whether or not you believe there is a Family of Dark or not, humanity will experience a very difficult year as everything accelerates. It's up to us to change the old paradigm and create a higher vibration for Earth. We can create an opportunity to transcend third-dimensional reality and explore the corridors of time and space. It's our task to heal ourselves on our journey along those corridors. We are facing the greatest spiritual test of all time—will you be a human who is service to self or service to others?

There are some hard realizations ahead, but there are a few great miracles along the road. For some of the evil ones, they will experience learn how they've contributed to hurting humanity. These times will be astounding—with a greater opportunity to eradicate fear and control from the planet. Connect your Heart to the Galactic Center, and then bring it back to the Earth's heart chakra. Transmit the frequency of love.

A great number of souls will leave at this time. It is not a random act, but a timely agreement made before each soul was born. Honor those that left and know that they will return at another time in the future. Nothing ever dies!

Humans are evolving ambassadors of Light. There is no one on Earth at this time who isn't impulsed to evolve into a higher state of being, even those who misguide and control dark souls who have forgotten how to love and what it means.

When you operate in the frequency of love, nothing is impossible. Others will want to know about this higher frequency that you radiate.

How will you measure up to the changes? Will you help and comfort your friends who are losing their jobs, their homes, their businesses due to COVID-19 and the mandates. Will you freak out as Earth makes bigger changes in her geology? Will you be an inspiration and stay calm and collected, knowing Earth must evolve too? Realize that you are needed, every one of you, to bring about this incredible new world with your love, compassion, and kindness to your fellow human.

Love is Light. To access LOVE, you must access the Light within you. It has always been within you, but you have forgotten and believed it existed outside of you. You were created from the Light and Mind of God. LIGHT is knowledge provided by the sun for our world to trigger our DNA. That's what the celestial being asks of us—recognize your DIVINITY!

The message is clear—Other Worldly beings and celestials are here to awaken human consciousness on a grand scale, and then our planet and all life will be forever transformed, and we will be allowed to travel throughout the galaxies as a member of the Galactic Federation—it does exist!

Along with us, there are multi-verses with multi-varieties of beings here to guide us and help us evolve through the most difficult and dangerous period on Earth. Like us, there are an infinite number of beings seeking the Light in different stages. Some are babies, some are in the kindergarten stage and others are far beyond college.

The higher beings await the glorious time when we discover our God Power.

The awakening of conscious awareness is unstoppable now and will be like the hundredth monkey. A time will come when people pay more attention to nature and all life and care for Earth rather than destroying everything. Take time to spend more time in nature. Walk among the trees, plants, rivers, oceans, lakes and speak to Mother Earth—she is alive. There are signs and omens in nature. Sleep on the ground, walk barefoot on the Earth, and feel the energy coursing through the planet. Smell the flowers, listen to the sounds of the animals and the insects toning to balance the energy grid, slow down and live in the moment. Climb a mountain and experience the incredible energy. Go on a Vision Quest like the indigenous people do—but bring water and supplies and be one with your environment. Study the stars and experience the Moon's cycles like the ancients did when the moon affects every aspect of our life—the ocean tides, animals, and women's monthly cycle. For all, the dark of the moon was a time to incubate ideas, record your dreams for signs, and be still.

Don't dwell on dark things happening now and in the future. The future is still forming and ever-changing. Live for the moment.

To heal the insanity, instability, anger, hate, and seeming uncertainty of these troubled times, you must learn to heal yourself first. Learning to manage energy will be your lesson and is one of the reasons you are here at this period in history. You must learn to stop blaming and accept your part in creating your reality. Transmute victimhood and you will find self-empowerment. As the energy on Earth accelerates, billions of people will awaken from their slumber. Just by opening up your heart and mind, you can create a safe, loving, and peaceful world. Acts of kindness and respect for all life will change the course of Earth.

Be brave in the monumental changes coming to our planet, speak your truth, but don't proselytize. Eventually, those who lag behind in knowledge will catch in an epiphany moment of Light. And most of all...*Human-up glorious Beings of Light, you are infinite.*

Betsey Lewis

DEAR FUTURE GENERATIONS, SORRY!

BY BETSEY LEWIS

Dear Future Generations, Sorry!

I speak for countless of us today. We are sorry for the mess we left you in our timeline. We abused our planet with overfishing, pollution of our precious waters in lakes, rivers, and oceans, and caused countless creatures to become extinct, and we continued to use fossil fuels instead of finding more natural energy sources that wouldn't harm Mother Earth. I'm sorry that you will never see the pristine waters that once existed on planet Earth, the incredible animals that once lived on the Earth and in the oceans. We are sorry how we destroyed the beautiful and life-giving rainforests by cutting and burning them to the ground. We forgot why trees were placed on the planet by removing carbon dioxide from the air and giving us oxygen to breathe. Now the rainforests are miles of desert sands, a great many creatures have are now extinct and most of our water is polluted and undrinkable. We forgot that every living thing has consciousness and should be honored and respected because we are all connected in ways we could never comprehend.

Dear Future Generations, we didn't think of you, and how we were horrible examples of how to behave like adults. We told you, "Don't do as I do, do as a say," and you became confused. Instead of teaching you to love one another, we taught you bigotry, hate, and violence. We destroyed our history but learned too late that without a past we have no future. I'm sorry that we created useless wars that only destroyed lives. We should have paid more attention to nature and cared for the Earth rather than obsessing about endless wars.

Sorry, that we left you a world where your precious freedoms no longer exist and how freedom of speech that we took for granted is gone. We should have seen all the signs, but we were too involved in our own lives to see the truth. I'm sorry that we became devolved humans instead of enlightened spiritual beings. Instead of becoming peaceful, we continued to fight among ourselves and create wars because we believed our truth was the right one, but the truth was—no one was right! We no longer treated each other as glorious beings of God, but instead, we judged, berated, and rated everyone and everything in our world, instead of seeing God-consciousness in all.

Dear Future Generations, sorry it was more important to have our huge homes, fancy cars, and other material things to impress others while turning a blind eye to the homeless, the jobless, and the hungry masses. We should have been more altruistic to those less fortunate. We forgot we are powerful, spiritual beings first, and material possessions couldn't be taken with us after we are gone.

Sorry, Future Generations that we watched the American Constitution torn away and became lazy, self-centered, civically ignorant sheep. We ate toxic food, bought manufactured products no one needed, and turned an uncaring eye away from millions of people suffering and dying worldwide. We were thoughtless about you—Future Generations, to come. We should have listened when Native Americans warned us that what we do in the present will affect the next Seven Generations.

Instead of the United States of America, we became the Divided States of America because we listened to those who cared less about us and only wanted to control us. We forgot to love one another and respect each soul as magnificent sparks of God. We forgot that we create our destiny and future by our actions, our thoughts, and our words. We forgot that we have walked in another's shoes in the distant past. We were once paupers, slaves, kings, queens, gay, straight, men, women, white, black, yellow, and red, warriors, and soldiers in past lives and we will again be reborn into new bodies to grow, learn and love. You see, if we had believed in the fairness of our Creator and in Divine Order, your life would be joyous and peaceful now. There would be balance and harmony. Every soul must evolve back to the Source. That's how souls grow and learn.

Dear Future Generations, perhaps what I have written today is just a terrible nightmare that never happened. That humanity awakened in time to become the *Butterflies in the Hurricane* transforming the darkness on our planet into Light, where future generations will praise us for our courage and our strength to transform the dark into LIGHT. The choice is ours at this moment to reprogram the Matrix for a kinder and more compassionate world.

Betsey Lewis

BIBLIOGRAPHY

Clarke, Dr. Ardy Sixkiller, *Encounters with Star People*, and *Sky People*, Anomalist Books, San Antonio, TX 78209.

Cott, Jonathan, *The Search for Omm Sety,* Warner Books, New York, NY, 1989.

Dennett, Preston, *The Healing Power of UFOs,* Blue Giant Books, 2019.

Emoto, Masaru, *Messages from Water and the Universe*, Hay House; Original edition (July 1, 2010)

Fowler, Raymond, *The Andreasson Affair, Englewood: Prentice Hall, 1982, The Watchers,* New York: Bantam Books, 1990, *The Watchers II,* Newberg, Oregon: Wild Flower Press, 1995.

Harney, Corbin, The Way It Is, Blue Dolphin Publishing, Nevada City, Nevada, 1995.

Hill, Julia "Butterfly", *The Legacy of Luna: The Story of a Tree*, Harper One, reprint 2001.

Marciniak, Barbara, *Family of Light,* Bear and Company, Inc., Santa Fe, NM, 1999.

Martin, Malachi, *Hostage to the Devil*, HarperOne; Reissue edition (October 1, 1992).

McFadden, Steven, *Ancient Voices, Current Affairs: The Legend of The Rainbow Warriors,* iUniverse; 0 edition reprint (July 13, 2005).

McGaa, Ed, Spirituality for America: Earth-Saving Wisdom for the Indigenous: 2013, and Mother Earth Spirituality, Harper San Francisco, San Francisco, CA, 1990.

O'Brien, Cathy and Phillips, Mark, *Trance Formation of America,* Reality Marketing, Incorporated, Revised edition September 1, 1995.

Roberts, Jane, *Seth Speaks,* Bantam Books (January 1, 1981).,

Schaefer, Carol, *Grandmothers Counsel the World,* Trumpeter Books, Boston, MA, 2006.

Soll, David, *Empire of Water*, available only in Audible Audiobook.

Stanford, Ray, *Fatima Prophecy,* 1972, Inner Vision Publishing Co., Virginia Beach, VA.

Yallop, David, *In God's Name: An Investigation into the Murder of Pope John Paul I,* Basic Books; New Edition (April 9, 2007).

ABOUT THE AUTHOR

Betsey Lewis inherited her psychic gift from two generations of women in her family. At eight months old, she and her parents had a UFO encounter on a northwestern Idaho highway late at night. What unsettled her parents was they had lost two hours during the trip without a logical explanation. Then in 1982, best-selling author and MUFON investigator Ann Druffel regressed Betsey and her mom through hypnosis to that night and uncovered an abduction aboard a UFO by small gray aliens.

At age seven, Betsey encountered a UFO that followed her home from her elementary school. Shortly after the event, she began experiencing recurring dreams of disastrous Earth changes currently taking place worldwide.

In the 1970s, Betsey began investigating alien stories, UFOs sightings, cattle mutilations in Idaho, ancient archaeological sites in Louisiana, and Native American petroglyph sites throughout the Northwest.

In 2016, seven months before President Donald Trump was elected, Betsey had a vision of Trump taking the oath of office wearing a black overcoat and his wife Melania wearing a light-colored coat. Her vision came true like so many of her predictions and visions. Newsmax TV Media featured her Trump prediction on the web with other psychics who all predicted a Hillary Clinton win. Betsey was the only psychic to had foreseen Trump's election as President.

Betsey has appeared on numerous talk shows like Coast-to-Coast AM, Ground Zero, KTALK's The Fringe, Fade to Black,

WGSO AM radio in New Orleans, and other well-known talk radio shows. Betsey was a keynote speaker at the 2015 UFO Conference in Albuquerque, New Mexico. She has authored fourteen non-fiction books on Amazon and three fictional children's books.

To learn more about Betsey, her published books, her upcoming events, her intuitive readings, and her daily Earth News blog, visit **www.betseylewis.com**

Made in United States
Orlando, FL
12 July 2023

35005022R00126